Praise For *Widowish*

"In *Widowish*, Melissa Gould takes readers on her journey through grief in all its complexity, reminding us, in the end, of our endless capacity for love."

—Lori Gottlieb, *New York Times* bestselling author of *Maybe You Should Talk to Someone*

"*Widowish* is an unputdownable modern love story, the kind you don't ever want to end. Except when it does, Melissa Gould has given us a transformational tale of modern loss and how grieving doesn't always have to look the way we thought. One of my favorite grief memoirs to date."

—Claire Bidwell Smith, author of *Anxiety: The Missing Stage of Grief*

"No one gets through this life without suffering some kind of loss, and Melissa Gould shares her journey with honesty, humor, and surprising insights. I read it straight through and now want regular updates on her life. *Widowish* is going to break your heart in the best way possible. I love this book!"

—Annabelle Gurwitch, author of *I See You Made an Effort* and *You're Leaving When?*

"In *Widowish*, you can acutely feel Melissa Gould's struggle to maintain normalcy as her husband slips away. This book is a brave and powerful examination of all the 'shoulds' that sometimes get in the way of our forward movement and evolution. I found myself rooting for Melissa the whole time."

—Vanessa McGrady, author of *Rock Needs River*

widowish

widowish

A Memoir

MELISSA GOULD

Published by Little A, New York

www.apub.com

Amazon, the Amazon logo, and Little A are trademarks of Amazon.com,
Inc., or its affiliates.

ISBN-13: 9781542018784 (hardcover)
ISBN-10: 1542018781 (hardcover)

ISBN-13: 9781542018760 (paperback)
ISBN-10: 1542018765 (paperback)

Cover design by Caroline Teagle Johnson

Printed in the United States of America

First edition

For Joel, "no matter what occurs" . . .
And for Sophie, always.

CONTENTS

AUTHOR'S NOTE

Most names and identifying details have been changed to protect the privacy of individuals.

ONE

Make Him Better

Y our husband is critically ill," said a doctor in the cold hub of the ICU. There were three of them, in their white coats, refusing to look me in the eye.

Behind me, past a closed curtain, Joel lay in his hospital bed, his dark hair slightly disheveled, his green eyes closed, wearing nothing but a hospital gown. He was hooked up to an IV surrounded by tubes and wires.

Here, at the active nurses' station, phones were ringing; I sensed information being exchanged about patients all around us, but all I wanted was clarity about my husband's condition.

"What exactly are you telling me?" I asked. "We have a thirteen-year-old daughter. I don't understand what you're saying."

The infectious disease doctor, who days earlier had examined Joel from head to toe looking for a bite or a welt or *something* that might indicate the reason for Joel's illness but had found none, said, "Joel is gravely ill."

Gravely? A second ago he had said *critically*.

I didn't understand what was happening. It had been three days since Joel was alert and awake. Three days since my husband walked into the emergency room because of the flulike symptoms that had been plaguing him for nearly a week. I felt a sense of urgency. Joel's health had rapidly declined since the hospital admitted him, yet no one seemed to have a clue as to why.

I had experience with Joel being ill. He had been battling multiple sclerosis for a few years. But MS is not a disease people die from. It's a "quality of life" disease that can cause problems with balance, muscle control, and other bodily functions, but it does not typically leave a person in the hospital, noncommunicative and nonresponsive.

When I had arrived at the hospital that morning, I expected the doctors to share some positive or at least conclusive news with me. An explanation why Joel was so sick and what would make him better—a course of treatment. I thought the latest MRI or the various specialists conversing with one another would give us, give *me*, some definitive action to take that would help Joel recover from this mystery illness that landed him in the ICU. Instead, the doctors had me reeling with fear and uncertainty. If Joel was critically, no *gravely*, ill, couldn't they help him?

"We're in a hospital!" I screamed. "You're all doctors. If Joel is sick, make him better!" They exchanged side glances at one another; it seemed each one was silently willing the other to say what they couldn't bring themselves to tell me. The infectious disease doctor wiped his hand across his face. The head of the ICU covered his mouth with his hand and continued to stare at his feet.

Joel's MS doctor, who had no privileges at this hospital, but whom I had fought to get approval for so that she could at least evaluate his chart and talk to the other doctors, finally looked at me with tears in her eyes. "We don't think we can."

~

I first met Joel in 1987. It was in the lobby of Atlantic Records on Los Angeles's Sunset Strip, where we both worked. Joel was four years older than me, and this was his "real" job, while for me, it was my summer job during college. I knew immediately that he was someone I would like when I saw his long rocker hair, shorts, combat boots, and the Who T-shirt he was wearing. I knew it was love when he told me a joke a few days later. We were in his "office"—the mail room. I was sitting on the counter, my legs swinging beneath me; Joel was printing mailing labels when he stopped to look at me.

"Where do cantaloupe and honeydew go in the summer?" he asked.

"Where?" I said.

"*John Cougar Mellencamp.*"

He paused, waiting for my reaction, and a smile came to his face, his green eyes twinkling. I couldn't help but laugh. In fact I laughed so hard, I started crying. He laughed, too.

With that silly joke, I decided that I wanted to marry someone just like him one day. I never thought it would *be* him, but right then and there, he set the bar high.

He was cool. He was funny. He was Jewish.

It was a trifecta that had otherwise escaped me. I was in my first serious relationship at the time, and Joel was living with his girlfriend. While we shared an unmistakable connection, our friendship was platonic. At night we'd see each other at shows. During the day at work we'd hang out in the mail room, and he'd play his current favorite songs . . . "What's My Scene" by Hoodoo Gurus . . . "Alex Chilton" by the Replacements . . . "World Shut Your Mouth" by Julian Cope.

Having grown up in both New York and Los Angeles, I had been exposed to the arts at an early age and had eclectic taste in music. I could hold my own, but Joel was more than just a fan of music, he was a connoisseur. His knowledge extended far beyond top 100 hits, band lineups, and genres—he knew *everything*. He knew alternative music before it was called alternative. He knew B sides and obscure facts about recording sessions and aspiring musicians. He knew tour dates and which A&R reps signed what bands to which labels. He knew and saw bands before they even *became* bands. He understood everything about the business, and it was his knowledge, interest, and curiosity that gave him joy.

We would have lunch together almost every day. We would pile into his Volkswagen Karmann Ghia and head down the strip for tacos, or a quick run into Tower Records on Sunset Boulevard to check inventory or just hang out—sharing our favorite finds.

As summer came to an end, I knew that Joel was a lifelong friend. He continued working at Atlantic; I graduated college, where I got my bachelor of arts degree in English, and moved to New York City to work in the creative department of an ad agency. But after a few years, the promotion I was hoping to get went to someone else. My new boyfriend and I broke up. I knew I wanted to write; I just wasn't sure that advertising was for me. I thought I'd try my hand at screenwriting and decided to move back to Los Angeles. As soon as I arrived back home, my best friend from high school invited me to a Dodgers game.

I was never into sports but had been to Dodger Stadium once before. It seemed bigger than I remembered. I handed over my ticket and walked through the turnstile. I looked up briefly to get my bearings and immediately saw a familiar face looking at me. It was Joel. His green eyes met mine, and my heart suddenly surged in a way it never had before. I was barely back in town. My life seemed in flux. Had I run into Joel that same night at a club, for instance, seeing a band, listening to live music, it would have made much more sense. This seemed so out of context, so strange and surreal.

Joel and his friend walked over to us. Joel and I hugged; it felt like no time had passed, even though we hadn't seen or spoken to each other in a couple of years.

"This is so weird!" Joel smiled. "These aren't even my seats!"

"I can't believe I'm seeing you!" I said, laughing.

"When'd you get into town?" he asked.

"I literally just got back," I said. "I live here now. Again."

"Really? So New York didn't cut it?" But I couldn't answer. I was too shocked to see him.

"Come on." My friend tugged at my arm. "Let's find our seats."

"Is it OK if I give you a call?" Joel asked.

I wrote down my phone number on his ticket stub. Our fingers touched when I handed it back to him. It was as if the stadium was suddenly empty and it was just the two of us, taking each other in. I didn't want the moment to end.

"It's really great running into you," he said.

My friend and I left to find our seats, but when I turned around for one more look, Joel's eyes were still on me. He was smiling.

~

We had been married nearly ten years when Joel started having trouble with his legs. He had left to play in his weekly basketball game. I had a busy day of filming, then made dinner for our family of three, and finished off with our daughter Sophie's nighttime routine of bath, books, and bed. The kitchen was now clean, the dogs were asleep, and all was quiet. It was finally my cherished alone time. I poured myself a glass of wine, grabbed a handful of chocolate chips, and was planning on settling in with *The Real Housewives of New Jersey*, when I heard the front door open. I was surprised. Joel had been gone for only about thirty minutes.

"Hun?" I asked.

He walked toward me, deeply distressed.

"Something's wrong," he said. "My legs. They're not working. It's like I see the ball moving down the court, I tell my brain *go get it* but I can't."

It took me a moment to process this.

"What? What are you talking about? Are you in pain?" I asked.

"No. But it feels like I can't play ball anymore. I try but I just stand there watching everything happen around me. I can't move, no matter how hard I try."

None of this made sense. Joel was *healthy*. He was an active guy and physical exertion meant everything to him. He played basketball and softball at least once a week. He'd also play racquetball a few times a month and went to the gym every morning. He had an optimistic and sweet disposition, but this inability *to move*, this disconnect between his brain and body, was alarming.

He sat down, deep in thought. I sat down next to him, leaned my body into his. He looked at me.

"Something's wrong," he repeated. "Something's really wrong."

I put my arms around him.

"OK, well, if something's wrong, we'll figure out what it is."

Joel nodded in agreement, but I could tell that his mind was racing.

He started to meet with one neurologist after another, but because Joel looked like the picture of health, no doctor took his complaints seriously. He was young, not even forty-two. He had always maintained a healthy weight, he didn't smoke, he had no reason to be in a doctor's office. Each doctor visit was frustrating, and figuring out the cause of his issues took some time. But Joel was determined—he knew something was wrong, he felt it in his soul. Finally, a new neurologist did an MRI of Joel's back and saw a bulging disk. He prescribed physical therapy.

"It's not making a difference," Joel complained a few weeks into treatment. "Anyone my age who gets an MRI of their back is going to find out they have a bulging disk somewhere. It's bullshit!" He was suffering. Every week he'd show up for basketball, hoping for a different outcome, but then he'd be home early again. "I'm just going to stop for a while," he said. "Give my legs a break."

It was during this break from basketball that another symptom appeared—occasional numbness and tingling in his feet. Another MRI was ordered, one that would provide insight into anything that isn't typically seen in a healthy person. Sure enough, these results were different.

Joel was sitting in our home office one night. Sophie was having a bath.

"The doctor called," Joel said. "I need to tell you what's going on." I knew by the tone in his voice it was serious. I sat down in the chair across from him. "He gave me my MRI results."

"OK," I said. "We'll deal with whatever it is." But my voice started to crack, and I felt tears pooling up in my eyes. Joel looked at me, anger flashing across his face.

"Don't!" he said. "If you start to cry, I won't get through this!"

So I held myself back. I took another deep breath. I reached for his hand. He looked at me and said quietly, "There are two lesions on my brain, and one on my spinal cord. That means it's MS. I have MS."

A million thoughts swirled around my mind as tears started streaming down my face. I tried to wipe them away; I didn't want Joel to fall apart. He squeezed my hand harder.

"I'm scared," he whispered.

And then I really started to cry. I got up, and I hugged him. I held him tight.

I could still hear Sophie splashing around in the tub.

"I love you," I said to Joel, holding on to him.

"You," he said back quietly.

You was our shorthand. It was our call and response to *I love you*.

Joel's eyes started to tear up. Both of us knew about MS, and we knew it well. Not only did his father's best friend have it, but so did my dad, who at that time was mostly symptom-free. Joel and I just never put it together. It's like when you're looking for your keys for a half an hour and realize you've been holding them the whole time.

Of course it was multiple sclerosis. The problems with his legs, the tingling, the body feeling disconnected from the brain . . . we must have been in denial.

After that night, we tried to maintain normalcy—get Sophie up and ready for school, keep her on track. Joel went to work every day, but it was impossible for him to concentrate. We were in shock. Joel, typically an "up" person, was down in a way I had never seen. He was quiet, remote; he went inward.

"I don't want to end up in a wheelchair," he'd say. "I want to dance at Sophie's wedding . . . I want to travel as a family while I can still walk."

"You're going to be OK, hun!" I'd say. But neither of us was sure.

At the time, the actress Selma Blair was years away from announcing her diagnosis, but some celebrities had come out with the fact that they, too, had MS—Montel Williams, Jamie-Lynn Sigler, Jack Osbourne. In a weird way, we took comfort in this. Joel did not want to end up like Richard Pryor, Annette Funicello, or Teri Garr. They were the public faces of MS at its worst, and what we feared could be Joel's future.

MS is a complicated disease that impacts the central nervous system. Brain communication to the body breaks down due to damaged myelin (the "coating" that surrounds nerve endings), causing a host of symptoms, which for Joel at that time affected his balance and mobility. The progress of the disease, as well as its severity, is unpredictable and manifests differently in every single person diagnosed with it.

After waiting a few months, Joel was seen by a renowned MS specialist. Being in his care meant there was a team of support behind us. One doctor, who we liked very much, became Joel's point person. She was also the one who would be monitoring his medication. I went with Joel to every doctor appointment, and he started to keep a journal of his symptoms to review at every meeting. After some deliberation, we agreed that Joel would start on Copaxone, which at the time was considered one of the "better" drugs, believed to slow down the progression of MS and alleviate some of its symptoms. For Joel, this worked great for a number of years . . . He would give himself the prescribed dosage of one shot, three nights a week.

"Fuck you, MS!" he would say with each night's injection.

Ice . . . shot . . . Advil. That was the routine. We got used to it. There were good days and bad, for sure, but Joel was coping. The meds were keeping things at bay. Joel was active. He rode his bike to work, saw live music. He was living his life, and life was good.

TWO

Milestones

On a whim, shortly after we learned he had MS, Joel purchased a one-month series to a new yoga studio that had recently opened in our neighborhood. He was desperate to find something that gave him the same endorphin rush and physical workout as running up and down a basketball court. He had never done yoga but felt like he would benefit from a more holistic approach to exercise.

He came home from his first class beaming.

"It was great," he said. "Feel my shirt. It's soaked!" He loved how much he sweat and moved in ways he never had before. He was amazed that this particular studio played some of his favorite music during class.

"You could be in down dog listening to Kings of Leon and start flowing to the Pretenders," Joel said. "But by the time we're in Savasana, Elliott Smith could be playing!"

This kind of *anti-yoga* yoga spoke to Joel, and he loved it. We would practice together. He was able to do moves and flows I struggled with. He would sweat and make me laugh, and when we lay on our backs in Savasana, our index fingers hooked together across the wooden floor.

Years later, Joel began to *feel* like he had multiple sclerosis for the first time since his diagnosis. The Copaxone stopped working. Joel would leave for yoga and come home crestfallen.

"I had to spend the whole time basically sitting on my mat. I could barely move," he'd complain.

Reluctantly, he stopped going to class. He could no longer ride his bike because it took too much effort to pedal and stay balanced. There was a time in our lives when Joel would go to concerts several times a week. Now he could only go if he had a seat—standing for hours was impossible. Without the ability to exercise, without the ability to see and hear live music, the MS was robbing Joel of the things that made him *him*.

While the Copaxone had worked well for years, we learned that most MS drugs have a limited life span, and it was time to find a new medication. As with many medications for chronic diseases, the side effects can be severe. Joel and I would laugh about these—each one worse than the other. Like a ridiculous *Saturday Night Live* sketch, side effects might include *permanent brain damage . . . heart failure . . . thoughts of suicide . . .*

The list went on and on.

"Don't worry, hun," Joel said jokingly. "The worst that can happen is my tongue might swell and block my breathing. Or I could get a severe brain infection that could kill me. Good times!"

Yet, there was hope. New medications were being developed and put through trials all the time. We were optimistic that Joel could live his life without compromise once he got started on a new treatment.

Joel started on a new drug, but after a month it just wasn't helping. It was difficult for him to walk, to stay clear minded. He would do something simple, like empty the dishwasher, and it would make him so fatigued that he'd have to sleep afterward. He was suffering; there was nothing I could do to help, and Sophie was becoming more aware of her daddy's condition. Joel didn't want her to worry about him or make her feel that he was compromised in any way from being the fun and loving parent he had always been.

When Sophie was born, we lived in a small house in the San Fernando Valley. We loved that little house with the big tree that took up most of the backyard and a pool that had both a slide and a diving board.

Joel, Sophie, and our shepherd mix, Lucy, could often be found in the backyard together, Joel carrying Sophie as he tended to our plants, or holding Sophie high above his head as he gently went down the slide into the pool. By the time Sophie could walk, they also loved their time picking up after Lucy. Joel would be in his swim shorts and flip-flops carrying a poop bag and shovel. Sophie would have on a T-shirt and her little rain boots with her bare bottom exposed. She would march around, pointing out all of Lucy's poop so that Joel could scoop it up.

"There's one!" she'd scream in her little toddler voice.

"See any more?" Joel would ask.

She would search and squeal with each pile she found. Disgusting, maybe, but Joel loved it, and Sophie loved the time with her daddy.

Now that Sophie was thirteen, other than wanting to put purple streaks in her thick, long hair and begging for a new cell phone every now and then, the only issues we had with her were when we, specifically I, would offer to help with her homework.

One night, I called them both to dinner. Sophie said she had to finish an assignment first.

"Come eat, and then I can help you after dinner," I said.

She snorted as she took her seat. "Like you can help."

I just shook my head and sighed.

"Don't talk to your mother like that!" Joel said.

"Like what?"

"You're being rude," he said. "That's not OK."

"Whatever." Sophie shrugged.

Joel stood up. His legs were stiff.

"Go to your room, Sophie," he said. "I don't like your attitude."

"Hun, it's OK," I said to him.

"No! It's not OK. She can't talk to you like that!"

I tried to minimize it. "She talks to me like that all the time, I don't even hear it anymore."

"Exactly!" Joel said, frustrated. He held on to the counter for balance.

"If she doesn't care, then you shouldn't either!" Sophie yelled.

"Go to your room right now!" Joel grabbed Sophie's chair, attempting to pull it and her away from the table.

"Fine!"

Sophie stormed off to her room and slammed her door. This enraged Joel. He tried to follow her, but his legs simply weren't working. He looked like he was walking on stilts. Joel yelled after her, "And do not come out until you apologize!"

With no warning, he collapsed to the floor. His legs could not even bend. It happened so quickly and unexpectedly that I gasped. I had never seen him like this, so frail and fragile. I rushed to his side and tried to help him up.

"Don't!" he yelled, pushing me away. He managed to get up somehow. "It's not OK for her to talk to you like that!"

"But your legs—" I said.

"Don't!" he yelled again.

With tremendous effort, like the Tin Man in need of oil, he made it to our bedroom. I didn't follow. I knew he didn't want me to.

So I stayed quiet.

And that's how it went. Joel's health got worse. It started to affect him not just physically, but emotionally and psychologically as well.

We would typically talk about everything. The extremely personal, married-couple variety of conversation (*Did you go today?*), to the more mundane (*Did you find that thingy for the thing?*), but the one topic that we suddenly stopped talking about was the most important—his health.

I decided to call Joel's mother.

"I need help, Nancy," I told her. I didn't want her to worry, but she needed to know the MS was starting to affect Joel. I also knew that keeping it to myself was becoming too much for me. Things turned bad so fast, and those closest to us didn't know or understand just how serious our situation was.

"It's Joel. He's just been sort of depressed lately. He feels like his legs aren't working that great."

"Oh no!" she cried.

"It's probably just a flare-up." I tried to minimize it, but I had no idea how long this *episode* might last. I also understood that no mother, no matter how old their child, wants to hear that their child isn't doing well. "Maybe you can call and check in on him and make us dinner every now and then?"

"Oh of course. I'll do that. You know I will," she said.

Nancy loved cooking for us, even when we didn't know if she was still a vegan or back to eating meat or just gluten-free or no sugar. When Nancy came to visit, she would bring us knickknacks and doodads she had picked up at various yard sales. These are the things that made her happy but were torturous to Joel and me. Nothing she ever touched would go to waste. It could be a broken piece of colored glass, old wrapping paper, a cigar box. Nancy would try to find a place for it in her home—the same home that Joel grew up in. She had so much stuff everywhere that Joel used to joke, "If we go to my mom's, don't put our keys down anywhere. We won't be able to find them when we want to leave."

Joel's parents, like mine, were divorced. So I made a similar call to Joel's dad. "Please, Hal. If you could meet him for lunch, even once a week, it could help."

Joel and Hal were close. They spoke on the phone often, and when he retired Hal rented some space in Joel's office just to have a place to go every day. This was something that Hal's wife, Rita, encouraged.

Joel was in his twenties when Hal and Rita got married, and she and Joel had a nice rapport. We all did.

I told Hal that I thought Joel was depressed because of the MS.

They had a typical father-son relationship. In large part it revolved around sports. They went to Dodgers games together, Lakers games. Joel was Hal's pride and joy. Hal looked at Joel the way Joel and I looked at Sophie. His whole being would light up whenever Joel walked into the room.

"Oh sure. I'll give him a call tomorrow. How's that?" Hal offered.

"Perfect," I said.

Joel's sister, who lives in Northern California, also suffers with an autoimmune disease. By the time Joel was diagnosed with MS, Andrea had been living with lupus for nearly twenty years. Andrea was stoic. We once went to visit her and her family while she was in the midst of a flare-up and recovering from shingles. *Shingles!* She still managed to trek literally across the entire city of San Francisco in one day. She didn't complain once.

I called Andrea to let her know that her older brother wasn't in great shape. They had their compromised health in common. In some ways, when Joel was diagnosed it brought them closer. Andrea, too, said she would check in on her big brother.

A few months earlier, both of our families had come to town for Sophie's bat mitzvah. It was a *Big Deal*. Friends and family flew in from around the country. Like a big wedding, the celebration took up the entire weekend. There was a rehearsal dinner the night before, the ceremony itself followed by a huge party, then a family brunch the day after. Planning the event took up most of the year, and Sophie spent several years of Hebrew school preparing for it. I was totally unfamiliar with the rituals of a Jewish education. I was born Jewish and knew what the holidays were, but my home was only Jewish in the cultural sense. My mother, in fact, favored celebrating Christmas over Hanukkah.

While Sophie's bat mitzvah was a magical weekend, it was obvious that Joel wasn't feeling well. It was tiring to have so many activities planned. He tried to overcome his exhaustion and overall discomfort. He was so thin! His walking was labored. So while it was a happy and joyous occasion, I noticed Joel's health was taking a turn. In photographs from that day, Joel is smiling, so proud, so thrilled—but I can see the distress in his eyes and the aches and pains he was feeling.

In a discreet lean toward me during the ceremony, Joel whispered, "I don't know if I can make it."

I looked at him, unsure.

"I don't know if I can move my legs," he said.

We were on a raised stage, the bimah, and our friends and family filled the audience just below us. All eyes were on us. I didn't want to create a scene; neither did he.

The rabbi and cantor took turns with Sophie, who mostly led the service in both English and in Hebrew. I held Joel's hand. I had concern in my eyes and a smile on my face. I inhaled, worrying, but I didn't know how to divide my attention between him and Sophie.

When it was Joel's turn to read his speech, something parents do during the service to acknowledge their child's achievement, he gave me a nod.

"You OK?" I asked.

He got up slowly and steadied himself. He lumbered heavily across the stage to reach the podium. His legs, he later told me, felt like they had metal braces on them.

I am guilt ridden thinking about that now. *Why didn't I help him?* It would have been so easy! My arm looped through his, my hand on his shoulder or wrapped around his waist. *I could have helped him!*

But I sat still. I did nothing.

Later, my sister mentioned to me that she could tell Joel was having trouble walking. Some of our closest friends, however, didn't notice at all. After the ceremony, miraculously, Joel felt better. Which is how MS seems to work. It's totally unpredictable.

At the celebration, Joel was raised in the chair during the hora—one hand held high in the air in triumph and the other holding on to the seat for dear life. He was happy. Friends came up to us, congratulating us, saying, "Mazel tov!" We worked hard to create a special night for all of us but mostly for Sophie. Her name was spelled out in lights, and the DJ created a dance list of songs of her choosing. She invited close to seventy friends while Joel and I, similarly to our small wedding, had a combined fifty guests including our friends and family. There were passed hors d'oeuvres, a massive buffet with chicken fingers for the kids, and salmon with lemon and capers for the adults. An ice cream bar with overflowing toppings was served for dessert.

"You did it, hun!" I said to Joel as we kissed on the dance floor. He had even managed a daddy-daughter dance with Sophie.

"I don't know what happened," Joel said, elated. "It's like God gave me the strength to get through the day. I didn't think I would."

I wrapped him in a hug. "You were great!"

The bat mitzvah was a snapshot of who Sophie was at thirteen years old. She was confident, articulate, and happy. Happy in the way that every parent wants their child to be. It came from within. She glowed with self-confidence and a sense of well-being. She was safe in the world with her feet firmly planted, and she had all the love we had to give to her and her alone.

We were overcome with pride and joy. But in the few quiet moments I had that weekend, my concern over Joel grew. It had been a rough year so far, and I saw no signs of that letting up. Joel's whole demeanor was different. Physically he appeared gaunt. His mood was muted. The MS was getting hard to ignore.

With Joel's fiftieth birthday coming up, we thought a change of environment would be nice. We decided to book a vacation to Cabo San Lucas. Joel always said he preferred Mexico to Hawaii. "The flight is shorter, it doesn't cost as much money, and the food is better." The resort we chose was gorgeous and had multiple pools with swim-up bars, plenty of places to eat and relax, and access to a swimmable beach. We were very content on the huge, bed-like chaises that lined the beach. We were protected from the sun inside our little cabana that also had fans and water misters to battle the heat. We'd settle in with our chips and guacamole and our newspapers and magazines. Sophie had Joel's iPad, and we were all content to do nothing. Still, Joel wasn't feeling well. He retreated to our room one afternoon, mumbling something about work. And while I knew that heat exacerbates the symptoms of MS, after a few hours I called him from one of the phones by the pool. "Hun, come back to the beach. Sophie and I miss you."

Half an hour went by before I spotted him on the huge circular staircase that went from the resort rooms down to the pools and beach. I didn't recognize him at first. He wore a wide-brimmed hat, and dark sunglasses covered his face. He looked so frail! He struggled making it down the stairs, holding on to the railing for support as he slowly managed each step. I hid my tears behind my sunglasses.

The next day was better. It wasn't as hot, the ocean not as choppy. Sophie wanted to go in, so Joel offered to take her. I went down with them and watched from the shore. There are no lifeguards on the beaches in Mexico, and everywhere you look signs warn of a strong undertow. After a while, Sophie swam back to shore easily. Joel was still in the water.

"That was so fun!" she said as I gave her a towel.

"What's Daddy doing?" I asked her, trying not to sound concerned. He was swimming toward shore but sort of bouncing around the waves, like a cork floating in water.

"The water is so nice," Sophie said, "he probably doesn't want to come out."

But I could tell that Joel could not find his footing, even in the shallow waters. The waves kept knocking him over, and he was trying hard to find his way to shore. Sophie was laughing, thinking that Joel was exaggerating his efforts. I probably laughed, too, until I realized it wasn't a joke.

"No fair," I told her. "You guys went in without me. I'm going in with Daddy."

The minute I swam past the break, I got pulled under. The water wasn't deep, but the undertow was shockingly strong. I managed to reach Joel.

"You OK?"

"Yeah. It's just hard to get out of this."

I pushed Joel into a wave that carried him past the break. I met him and tried to make it a lighthearted moment by carrying him the way a groom carries his bride over the threshold to their new home. I didn't want to embarrass him for needing help. Nor did I want Sophie to notice that Joel could not have made it out on his own. We didn't want Sophie to know how much Joel was really struggling, and how frightening that dip in the ocean really was. Of course, she knew he had MS. She saw him take his medication and knew that he got tired at times or that his legs were bothering him. But it didn't affect her daily life. She was protected from her father's limitations, even when he was struggling to get out of the ocean.

We spent the rest of our trip by the pool.

We celebrated his birthday at a beautiful restaurant at an organic farm that reminded us of California wine country. We ate delicious food, toasted Joel's fiftieth with margaritas in a truly magical setting, but the trip didn't offer the reprieve we had hoped it would.

We were ready to go home.

THREE

Uncertainty

Two months after we got back from Cabo, I took my husband to the emergency room. For two days Joel had a high fever, most of which he slept through, but he suffered from chills and disorientation when awake. He was lucid when we made the decision together to take him to the hospital. He walked in himself. He didn't need a wheelchair or my assistance. Neither of us was versed in hospital etiquette, but I thought we would admit him and that he'd be home a few days later.

Even though the MS had been hitting him hard, fever and chills didn't *seem* like MS. We didn't understand what was happening to make Joel so sick. They took blood and urine samples, but the test results were all negative or inconclusive. With Joel clearly not well, hours later he was moved out of the ER and into a hospital room.

The new medication Joel had started months earlier still didn't seem to be helping. He was so tired of being sick. He had been in constant communication with his doctors from the minute we got back from Mexico. The day we arrived home, he sent this email. In part it reads:

> Dr. K, I've been going downhill rapidly since the beginning of the year . . . I'm getting worse daily.

It's very difficult for me to walk, standing still is also a challenge. I'm afraid that by the time the new meds kick in, I may lose my ability to walk.

Around the time of this email, his doctors ordered another MRI. They discovered one particularly bad lesion on his brain that they were convinced was the reason for the yearlong flare-up. If that lesion could start to heal, they believed Joel would start feeling more like himself again. They prescribed steroids.

Steroid treatment was used as a protocol to provide an energy boost and to help prevent the symptoms of the flare-up from getting worse. A nurse came to the house every morning for five days to administer the steroids through an IV. Because steroids lower the immune system, it's advised to stay indoors with little to no outside contact to avoid catching random germs and/or infections. The only people Joel saw that week were Sophie, the nurse, and me. We washed our hands constantly, and I got in the routine of using antibacterial wipes on every surface any of us came into contact with.

Joel had taken oral steroids before and they were quite effective, but this round of steroids, which were exponentially stronger, didn't seem to help. The doctors thought *another* round of steroids, to be administered in the coming months, might do the trick. But Joel was frustrated. It had been a very difficult year with new symptoms appearing constantly. Medications meant to alleviate his discomfort did little to help. All of this was affecting his job. He would oftentimes work from home, which helped, but he was feeling desperate for relief of any kind. He changed up his already healthy diet and started acupuncture, but neither option offered any consolation.

His doctors were kind and compassionate, but because Joel was easygoing and otherwise healthy, I encouraged him to be the squeaky wheel so they could understand just how much he was truly suffering. Two weeks after Joel sent his first email, he sent another:

Good morning, Dr. K. I know you're busy but as a patient going through a very rough time, I need some attention. This has been a horrible year for me and I'm trying to get as many answers as possible for my own peace of mind. I've started an acupuncture and anti-inflammatory diet regime. The IV infusion really didn't have any effect on me. I'd like to wait until mid-October before revisiting the next round.

But by October, Joel would be in the hospital. We would have no idea why.

~

"What's happening with you and Ellie?" Joel asked me one night as I washed my face.

He sat on the edge of the tub, his matchstick legs awkwardly lying straight out in front of him. He could no longer bend them comfortably.

"We're trying to figure it out," I said.

Ellie and I had become friends through our kids' elementary school. Her company had relocated, forcing an end to her career in TV news. The Writers Guild was going on strike. This meant my long-standing career as a TV writer was in flux. Both Ellie and I were looking to make a change. We decided to start a high-end concierge service for expecting parents, but we ended up becoming a go-to source for media in the Hollywood maternity space. This meant that when Brad Pitt and Angelina Jolie had a baby, Ellie and I would talk to the morning shows about how they might fill their nursery. This attention resulted in not just one but two different reality shows being developed around our company. We both saw ourselves as behind-the-scenes TV people. We weren't necessarily meant to be on-camera talent, but that's how things evolved.

It had recently become clear, though, that the reality shows weren't going to happen. We had no clients. We had to face the fact that as successful as we were from a publicity and public relations standpoint, our company bank account was empty. We were influencers at a time when that term didn't exist. We didn't know how to monetize what we did. Ellie and I were starting to accept that it was time to close up shop.

"What about your movie?" Joel asked.

A year prior, when our first reality show didn't get a green light, I had tiptoed back to the world of TV and sold a movie idea to Disney Channel. I had written the script and gone back and forth with the network on notes and rewrites. It was now in the hands of new writers with the hopes it would get a production order. If it did, I would get a financial bonus, residuals down the road, and most importantly, our health insurance would be extended by at least another year or two. If it didn't get a green light (it didn't), I had already made my money.

I knew why Joel was asking. I turned to face him.

"I need to bring in some steady income again," I said.

"That would help," he said. "I'm sorry, hun. I just . . . I'm not sure how much more I can work. I don't . . . ." His voice cracked. This was killing him. I sat down next to him. Buried my head in his shoulder.

"I just don't feel well. I can't keep working if I'm like this," he said, welling up. "I'm sorry."

"It's OK," I said. I rubbed his back. "It's OK. We'll be OK."

But my mind was racing.

Joel is suffering. He's getting worse. I need to do something to help.

The next day I started calling agents and producers I had worked with in the past. I sent emails and set up lunches. I had an idea for a half-hour show and decided to write that script on spec and use it as a sample to get hired on an established show. If I could garner interest in my spec and someone was interested in producing *that*, great, but a staff writing job was the goal. The work and income would be consistent.

I worked on my idea. I wrote the script over a few months and felt good about using it as a sample. I had planned to start sending out my script the following Monday.

But that was the weekend I took Joel to the emergency room.

Once he was settled in his hospital room—*as if it were a hotel!*—I wanted to get home and disinfect the house and do laundry. I didn't want Sophie or me to *catch* whatever Joel had. We needed to stay healthy.

I don't want Sophie to worry.

I don't want Joel to get worse.

What is happening to my husband?

That first night Joel was in the hospital, Sophie slept in bed with me. I tried to stay positive when I told her before lights out, "You'll spend tomorrow with Nana and Papa doing something fun! Then I'll meet you at the hospital in the afternoon so you can visit Daddy."

"OK," she said with a yawn.

This seemed like a perfectly reasonable plan.

I returned to the hospital the next morning with Joel's pajamas and some of his favorite foods. I thought we would hunker down together and hang out . . . but when I got there, I couldn't believe what I saw. Joel was sitting up in his bed, but he wasn't alert. His brow was creased, and he seemed to be in distress and speechless. He knew that I was there, but he didn't acknowledge me. He was out of it in a way I had never seen, and I didn't know what to do. Doctors came and went, and nurses took his vital signs. It was hard to take in. None of it made sense. I was scared.

Two days before, Joel had been home. He was feverish, but we were joking. He lay in our bed, wrapped in blankets and propped up on pillows, when he said he wanted me to put him out of his misery.

"Just kill me, hun. We need to figure out how you can do it, though, without getting caught."

I sat down next to him and smoothed a cool cloth on his forehead.

"Yeah, I don't want to go to jail," I said, smiling.

"Exactly. What would happen to Sophie?" he wondered. "We need a good plan."

"How about I smother you with a pillow?" I offered.

"That could work," he said thoughtfully. He looped his pinky finger with mine. I kissed his hand. We started laughing because we had many conversations like this. It was because of the MS that we had both serious and fantastical ideas about the end of life.

"If I die," Joel would say, "just make sure you marry a nice guy so that Sophie has a good father figure around."

"Ooh, I can't wait," I'd say. Then I'd add my favorite line: "Jeff Tweedy will be a great stepfather."

Joel would then say, "I approve."

The joke was that I could name anyone of the moment: Jeff Tweedy (lead singer of the band Wilco) . . . Howard Stern . . . Marc Maron . . . Anyone who both Joel and I liked for whatever reason. Once when we were at Trader Joe's, a nice employee found something for us that wasn't on the shelves. Joel smiled at me, pointed to the guy, and said, "I approve."

Even when it seemed like he was at his worst, we didn't think he was going to *die*. We found relief in the comedic and absurd. It's how we coped with our lives taking a turn neither of us saw coming.

Nothing that was happening in the hospital now, however, was funny. By Sunday night, Joel was nonresponsive and noncommunicative. I was overwhelmed, confused, and terrified. I was worried for myself, worried for Sophie. The person I needed most was unable to help me . . . and I had no idea how to help him.

Sophie slept with me again the next night. It was early October. She had just started eighth grade. There was so much to look forward to! She was cast in the school talent show that had rehearsals for weeks. Having been in previous years' musical theater productions, she was determined to get a *real* part this year. There were school trips planned to San Francisco and New York City, not to mention middle school graduation and then high school. It was a fun time in her young life. She had good friends whom she loved, and she was excited for what lay ahead. I didn't want any of that to change.

"Daddy's going to be OK," I told her that Sunday night.

"When do you think he'll be home?" She was concerned about him making it to the talent show the following week.

"Hopefully in time to see you perform!" I tried to sound hopeful, but I was at a loss. While she slept, I called the hospital. It was the middle of the night.

"He's still got a fever," the night nurse sweetly told me.

"Has he been able to talk at all?" I asked.

"Not yet," she said. "Don't worry, honey. We have your number. Call as many times as you'd like, but we'll keep you updated."

"Thank you," I said as I hung up.

I was too tired and scared to cry. My heart was racing. I watched Sophie sleep on Joel's side of the bed. I wanted to hold her, but I didn't want to wake her up. I wanted to assure her that everything was going to be OK. But I wasn't sure it would be.

FOUR

No Matter What Occurs

By Monday Joel had been moved out of his hospital room and admitted to the intensive care unit. He remained noncommunicative and nonresponsive. He was breathing on his own, but there was concern over the strength of his lungs. The doctors started saying things like, "Your husband is critically ill." But no one could tell me why or how things had turned so bad so quickly.

I started making phone calls to friends. My close friend Mimi, who is incredibly responsible and organized, convinced me that I needed some help. I told her where she could find the key to my house, and she began coordinating with some other friends. One day I came home to a house full of flowers. The next, to a fully stocked fridge of ready-made meals. I was typically the type of person who handled things on my own, but something inside me succumbed. People wanted to help us. I let them.

My mother lived nearby and was devastated by what was happening. She loved Joel and offered to help in any way she could. She spent time with Sophie, cooked for us, and made herself available.

My dad and stepmom, Elisabeth, who live in New York, happened to be in Northern California on vacation. We had plans to meet them in the central coast the following week. But with Joel so sick, they cut short their trip to the wine country and headed straight for Los Angeles.

Joel's dad was a constant presence, and I spoke to Joel's mother, Nancy, every night. It was difficult for her to see Joel so incapacitated, and as a mother, I understood completely. I sent emails to Joel's employees and closest friends to let them know that Joel was out of commission for at least a few days, maybe a week.

Sophie continued to sleep with me every night. I would take her to school, which had always been Joel's job, then head straight for the hospital. People offered rides, but I wanted to be there to pick her up every day like normal. I kept her in a bubble, reassuring her that "Daddy is going to be OK. He must really need this rest." She seemed to understand. This went on for days.

When I think of Joel in the hospital on those fraught, early days, I try to forget about the tubes in his nose and mouth, the IVs connected to his arms, and the soft whir of machines that helped him breathe.

It wasn't like the movies where the bereft spouse cuddles in bed with their sick husband or wife, smoothing down their hair and kissing them on the lips. Between the tubes, wires, and machines, I couldn't get close to Joel even if I wanted to. I feared something would become disconnected or loose. I was anxious seeing him like that, being unable to touch him or get close. He couldn't tell me what he needed, what would make him more comfortable, or more importantly, how to help him.

I tried to speak to him but I felt self-conscious—there was a steady flow of people in the room—nurses, doctors, visitors. And Joel was there, but *he wasn't there*. I would lean over the plastic tubes, whispering in his ear:

"*You,*" I'd say.

"*I love you.*"

"*I'm here, hun!*"

The only thing I could offer was my love.

After we ran into each other at that Dodgers game, Joel and I would see each other at shows around town quite often. The girlfriend Joel had been living with when we met at Atlantic Records was now his wife. She was rarely at shows with him, and while Joel and I always had chemistry when we saw each other, I was focused on starting my career.

By then I was working at Walt Disney Television, writing and networking like crazy, and was determined to get a job as a TV writer. I answered my phone one day; it was Joel.

"Perfect timing!" I said.

"Really, why?"

"I'm moving to Seattle next week!" I told him about the writing job I had just accepted on a new kids' science show called *Bill Nye, the Science Guy*. I was thrilled.

There was silence on the other end of the phone.

"This is the part where you say you're happy for me. It's why I moved back to LA, so I could move to Seattle," I said jokingly.

"I'm happy for you," he said, "but you just got back from New York."

"I know. It's kind of crazy."

Again, there was silence.

"The thing is," he said, "I let you get away once. I'm not going to let that happen again."

"What do you mean?"

But I knew what he meant. Like a cartoon, Joel and I had hearts in our eyes that day we met, but the timing was always off.

"Go to Seattle," he said, and then with over-the-top theatricality, he added, "*Stay alive, no matter what occurs! I will find you!*" It was a serious and dramatic line from *The Last of the Mohicans* delivered by Daniel Day-Lewis's character.

We both started laughing hysterically. Nervous laughter, perhaps, but it was typical Joel. The side of Joel that made me love him even more every time he said something funny or with innuendo.

When I left for Seattle, I went with no commitment from Joel, and I wasn't expecting one. Our lives were separate—we had never been a couple. As much as I continued to long for someone *just like Joel*, I put all of those feelings behind me. My life was starting, and I couldn't wait. It was 1993. Seattle was *the* place to be. It was the epicenter of the biggest shift the music business had seen in decades—*grunge*. I was young and unencumbered . . . Kurt Cobain was still alive. I was writing on a TV show and still very connected to my love of music, which was entirely accessible to me. I was in heaven!

A few months later, Joel started a new job and was on tour with the metal band Anthrax. The weekend they rolled through Seattle, Joel called and asked me to meet him at the theater where the band was playing. I was excited to see him and catch up. But when I left work that night, he was standing outside the production offices waiting for me. My heart nearly burst out of my chest. I felt scared and excited at the same time.

"What are you doing here?!" I asked.

We stood there looking at each other. It felt like the world around us had stopped moving.

Joel walked toward me, reached for my hands. "I'm here because I can't live my life without you. I don't want to anymore."

A thousand thoughts swirled through my mind.

"What?" I asked. "You're married."

"We separated. Months ago. Right after you left."

I was stunned. "Really?" I couldn't believe that the man I pined for all those years was standing in front of me making this declaration.

"I love you. I want to be with you. Please tell me that's OK."

I stood there silently staring at Joel. But I was smiling. "I can't believe this," I said.

"I know. It's weird."

"Yes," I managed to say.

"Yes, this is weird, or yes that it's OK?"

"Yes," I said again. "Yes."

Joel smiled, took my face in his hands, and kissed me, deeply.

We didn't stop kissing the entire few days he was in Seattle. We were giddy with the fact that we were together. That we could hold hands and kiss and spend hours on end talking about life in a way that we never had before. Joel confessed that he was ready to make serious changes in his life, a life that he wanted to spend with me.

My world was rocked when Joel showed up in Seattle, and it was good that he left to finish up the tour. It gave us both the time we needed to sort out what was transpiring.

While I really loved Seattle, I wanted a TV writing *career* and to start a life with Joel. I knew that meant living in Los Angeles. When the Anthrax tour ended months later, Joel bought a one-way plane ticket to Seattle. Together we took our time driving my old BMW down the coast and back to Los Angeles. By the time we arrived, we were a bona fide couple.

~

In the ICU, I held Joel's hands, which alternated between freezing and feverish. I tried rubbing his feet with lotion, because they felt cold and dry, but the doctors stopped me from putting socks on them due to a concern that they would deregulate his already fluctuating temperature. Every day I was granting permission for another test, approval for yet another doctor to assess him, all while trying to make sense of what was happening. I wanted to ask Joel, no, beg him, *What should I do?!* I was afraid of making any decision for fear it was the wrong decision. I was trying to manage his care in the hospital and protect Sophie from the full extent of what was making her daddy so sick.

Our friends and family were scared and worried for us. I gave Joel's best friend, Greg, the task of updating a small but close group of friends so that I wouldn't have to answer every phone call, text, and email.

After just four days, the doctors told me that I should move Joel to the hospital where his MS team was. Because the diagnosis was unclear, so was the prognosis. The prevailing thought was that this *was* perhaps something to do with Joel's MS and/or his new medication. It became evident that while this hospital provided full-service medical care, they had done everything they could for Joel.

But moving Joel meant a commute to downtown LA. It was a logistical nightmare. How would I be able to be there every day *and* be available for Sophie? Why couldn't this hospital help him? Nothing made sense to me.

I spoke to Joel's dad about the move. Hal liked to tease that I never wanted to stray too far outside of the valley. "Melissa," he said, "I agree with the doctors. I know it will be tough for you, but let's move Joel downtown." Hal meant that as a joke—he was optimistic, but I wasn't.

What lay ahead was fraught with uncertainty. There was tremendous mystery surrounding Joel's condition. Cultures for a variety of viruses had been taken, and all of them came back negative. While they supported and encouraged it, the doctors were also concerned that he may not survive the transfer to the hospital downtown.

I called Joel's sister, Andrea.

"You really should come down here, sis," I told her. "Your brother is in bad shape."

She seemed shocked. "Really? Dad said I should wait. He said Joel's going to be fine in a few days, and it would be more meaningful to come when he's home."

I lost it. Tears started pouring out of my eyes. I yelled, "When he's home?! Andrea, I don't know when he's coming home! I don't know what shape he'll be in when he's home! *If* he comes home! Why would your dad tell you Joel's going to be fine—that's not what they're telling me!"

I felt very alone. Was Hal in denial or was I overreacting? As Joel's wife, I was privy to Joel's struggles. I had only just reached out for help recently. People, even close family, didn't understand the extent of how the MS was affecting Joel . . . and us as a couple.

"I can't walk, I can't shit, I can't fuck," Joel would lament. "What's the point of living?"

As I struggled with everything that was going on, Ellie had offered to call the rabbi. "This is what she does," Ellie insisted. "When someone gets sick, you let the rabbi know."

Sophie's bat mitzvah had been only a few months before, so I felt very comfortable with Rabbi Hannah. Still, as much as I wanted to embrace my Judaism, particularly around the bat mitzvah, I had grappled with the realization that after all of it—the joyous weekend of bat mitzvah–related family activities, as well as the months leading up to it—I was simply Jew-*ish*. Outside of my liberal and cultural connection to Judaism, I just didn't connect. But I knew Joel would have welcomed a visit from the rabbi without hesitation.

Judaism was always a part of his life, and it was important to him. He grew up in a Reform Jewish home, went to temple, celebrated and understood all of the holidays. I knew exactly where in the closet he kept his talit—a prayer shawl that men wear on special Jewish occasions. It was on his shelf of prized possessions, next to his *Big Lebowski* bobblehead and the rogue fly baseball he caught at a recent Dodgers game. That was one of the best days of Joel's life. The ball came fast and unexpectedly in his direction, and he caught it barehanded and effortlessly.

I said to Ellie, "Sure. If you want to call the rabbi, go ahead."

The next day, Rabbi Hannah came to the hospital. I was crying and hovering over Joel when she entered the room. Greg and Hal were watching the Dodgers in a World Series playoff game.

"Turn on the game!" Our friends were calling and texting me. "He'll want to see it!" They weren't wrong, he *would* want to see it. His beloved Dodgers hadn't won the World Series since 1988. It seemed possible that they would go that far again. The game was on, but Joel had no idea.

I asked for some privacy with the rabbi.

"I don't know what's happening to him," I cried to her.

Because we didn't know how things got so bad so quickly, the doctors couldn't predict what recovery might look like. But the prognosis wasn't good. They started to use percentages about his recovery. They would say things like, "It'll be slow, but he could make a fifty percent recovery. Maybe more." Math was never my strong suit. But even I understood that the chances for a *full* recovery were low. Especially because Joel was admitted at less than 100 percent capacity.

"I know this is difficult," Rabbi Hannah said. "We are all praying for him."

"I appreciate that." I was comforted by her presence, but I struggled with how to tell her my most recent thoughts.

I looked at Joel: his eyes were closed, he was wearing a hospital gown, the ubiquitous tubes were monitoring his vital signs.

Finally, I confessed. "I'm just not sure we're all praying for the same thing."

I didn't know what I was praying for anymore. *Joel's recovery? To what end?* I hadn't heard his voice or felt him respond to my touch in days. Joel was tired of living with MS. He had felt compromised every day of his life for the past ten months. He was worried and lived in fear of losing his dignity. I wanted him whole. I wanted him as I had always known him—vibrant, alive, healthy.

But saying that out loud, admitting that I wasn't sure what I was praying for, I was afraid I would be struck down by God on behalf of all Jews and good people everywhere. Or that I would at least feel some judgment from the rabbi.

How can I not be accepting of prayers for my husband's recovery?
How can I not be accepting of people wanting Joel to get better?

Rabbi Hannah took my hands in hers. "Melissa," she said, "what we are praying for is Joel's complete and full recovery." I nodded, wanting to believe that a complete and full recovery was even possible.

My tears were flowing when I whispered, "And if that doesn't happen?"

She looked at me and said, "Then we pray for whatever is in Joel's best and highest good."

I took in those words carefully.

There was no reproach. No shock. No criticism.

Those words opened a door for me. I was finally able to exhale.

FIVE

Quality of Life

I gave the OK to move Joel downtown. Hal and I followed the ambulance during the transfer, and my best friend of twenty-five years, Jillian, met us at the new hospital.

I asked the head of *that* ICU, "Is my husband in a coma?"

"Well," the doctor said, trying to explain, "I mean, coma is an umbrella term. He's nonresponsive and noncommunicative, so yes, you could say he's in a coma." This didn't seem to faze her, but her nonchalance left me in shock.

My husband is in a coma.

I turned to Hal. "Did you think he was in a coma?"

"No, but I think he'll be OK. I think they can help him here."

Hal's optimism was admirable. Whenever I looked his way, he'd be smiling, hopeful. Or maybe it was some level of denial that Hal used to cope. I wasn't wired that way.

Although this was a different hospital and we were dealing with the same dire circumstances, it did feel hopeful that Joel's MS specialists were here. His doctor was able to rule out that certain viruses known to be related to MS and the new meds that Joel had been taking were causing this coma. I was happy to have Joel under the watchful eyes of his team. These doctors knew him as a person and not just as a patient.

They were familiar with his case, which gave us some confidence that *maybe* we would all come out of this slightly less scathed.

Sophie seemed OK. I tried to minimize any worry that I was feeling so that I wouldn't transfer my fears to her. It's not that I was holding back, but I had nothing concrete to tell her: "Daddy is in a coma, which means he's resting. His body is working really hard to fight off whatever is making him so sick."

"But he's going to be OK, right?" she'd ask.

"That's what they say. It's hard to know. It will be a slow recovery."

She took that at face value. I also didn't bring her to the hospital often. She didn't like being in the ICU, and I assumed visits were traumatic. Joel was surrounded by people who were very sick. Their ailments were visible. They were able to communicate their pain and discomfort. Joel wasn't.

Joel was also younger than all of the other patients by at least twenty years. He still had his dark and full hair, and his beard was growing in. He did not look like he belonged. But there he was. Tubes in his mouth, arms, and hands.

It had been over a week since I took him to the emergency room, and yet we didn't have more information. He had another MRI. A brain angiogram. A spinal tap. Several EEGs to monitor brain activity. More blood work. More cultures. The doctors kept asking me if Joel had a rash recently. They continued to circle the idea that this was a virus. But which one?

They ruled out anything bacterial, which meant antibiotics would not have helped. They ruled out cystic fibrosis. His liver function was normal but his brain activity was slow. Every day was another educated guess about his condition, and while I tried to stay positive, it was difficult. Joel was in a coma. If this was a virus, then there was no treatment. What they were doing was supportive care—keeping his lungs clear and feeding him. There was no specific infection they could treat. At this point, Joel's MS doctors checked in daily, but they took a back seat to the plethora of specialists who were all trying to figure out his mystery illness, which seemed to come from a yet-to-be determined virus.

I was inundated with calls and emails, and I had nothing definitive to share. I was waiting for the doctors to figure out how to make him better. I assumed they would.

My dad and Elisabeth were staying with us, which was helpful in every way. As glad as I was that Sophie was getting some grandparent love, I needed some of it, too. I went into their room one night while they were in bed watching TV. I sat on the floor at the foot of their bed and started to sob.

"I should have taken him to the hospital sooner," I cried. "I didn't know what to do. His fever was so high! But then it would come down when he took the Tylenol, so I thought he'd be OK. It was like that for days."

"You did the best you could," Elisabeth said. "Don't beat yourself up!"

"Really," my dad echoed. "Joel's in good hands. You couldn't have done anything differently."

But it all played in my head over and over. He had a high fever. But then he'd feel hungry and eat something. He was up. He was walking around. Then he'd get back in bed with a fever. We were laughing, telling jokes. I couldn't make sense of any of it.

Sophie's eighth grade class had made some get well cards, and I taped them to the machines around Joel's bed. Ellie's husband had visited Joel and brought in some family photos he put on the bulletin board. Joel's friend and business partner, Ben, came to visit one day and was astonished that I wasn't playing any music.

"You gotta bring some tunes when you come back," he said. "It's Joel we're talking about. Music will help him!"

I couldn't believe I hadn't thought of that myself. So the next day I brought Joel's iPod and hooked it up to some portable speakers. It was a great idea. All the doctors and nurses wanted to be in his room. We were vibrant and young. Joel still looked handsome.

My parents were able to join me at Sophie's talent show. They sat a few rows in front of me while I put on a brave face and sat in the back of the middle school auditorium. Sophie wanted to surprise Joel and me with her role. She initially downplayed it and said she didn't have much to do in the show, when in fact she was one of the masters of ceremonies. She was onstage most of the evening—confident, happy, and proud of herself.

I was entirely distracted. I kept thinking, *Joel should be here. What is happening to my husband? I miss him!*

I was also watching my phone. I was waiting for a call from our internist. He was our family doctor of the old-school variety—patient, thorough, and genuine in his concern. He had been in regular contact with Joel's doctors, and I wanted to hear his point of view on the prognosis.

My phone rang. I stepped outside.

"Melissa!" our internist said. "I'm sorry, dear. Joel is really very sick. How are you holding up?"

"Not great," I said.

"He's in excellent hands. If it's a virus, then it will be a slow recovery, but he can pull through. You need to stay strong for yourself and for your daughter. How is she?"

I could hear Sophie onstage telling a joke.

Joel should be seeing this.

I wiped the steady flow of tears streaming down my cheeks. "Sophie's doing OK," I told him. "Do you think it's a virus?"

"They've taken a lot of tests for all of the California viruses. The rapid results came back negative, but sometimes that can change. They will keep testing him, but we are going to have to wait and see. The MRIs show nothing new. Could be the MS, his medication. Probably is a virus, though. Let him rest. Go be with your daughter."

We hung up. There was no new information. Joel had been in the hospital for two weeks. By now, I knew that a healthy person could get a virus and not necessarily know it. It may seem like a mild flu or a cold. But to someone with a compromised immune system, like Joel, any of the viruses he was being tested for could be lethal. The doctors all believed, though, that because Joel was young and otherwise healthy, even if he did have a virus, he could recover, albeit slowly.

I went back into the auditorium. Sophie was center stage. There was applause and laughter. She was beaming.

~

Long before Joel was diagnosed with MS, we were dealing with another medical diagnosis: unexplained infertility. We had been trying to get pregnant since we moved to our second home near a coveted elementary school. Sophie was two and a half years old, and we wanted to fill our new house with more children and give her a sibling. We would vary between trying really hard for a baby, and at other times, just sort of trying. We both felt like we had time. I was in my midthirties, Joel was approaching forty, and other than us not getting pregnant, we were happy.

Joel was a partner in a music marketing company that he started with his friend Ben. His office was around the corner from our house. He would walk or ride his bike there every day and often come home for lunch so he could spend some time with Sophie. I had just wrapped my work as a writer and producer on *Lizzie McGuire*, a show that helped put Disney Channel on the map and gave meaning to the word *tween*. I was also doing some film writing work and pitching a movie. We were successful and busy. We both thought a baby would come when it was supposed to.

It didn't help that friends who had started their families when Joel and I had Sophie were now pregnant with their second or even third child. Just like the curiosity that came when Joel and I first lived together (*Think you'll get married?*) to questions about the wedding and beyond (*When are you going to start a family?*), now came the incessant and, in hindsight, insensitive questions about having more (*When are you going to make Sophie a big sister?*).

Sophie was at an age where she noticed that some of her friends had brand-new siblings at home or babies growing inside their mommy's tummies.

"Why don't they just get a dog?" she would say.

She was in no rush to become a big sister. And why would she be? Not only was she the center of our world, but she also had six doting grandparents. Two grandpas and four (*four!*) grandmas. She had an entire wing of the house to herself. As far as she was concerned, her sister was our dog, Lucy, her brother was our cat, Puddin', and she seemed very content to be the sole recipient of all of our love and attention.

But every month, as hopeful as I may have felt that *this* time I might be pregnant, we were met with the fact that we weren't. I would sometimes blame myself. I loved being a mom! But I also loved having a career. No matter how many times I drove through the gates of the Disney lot, I got a thrill. I loved being on set. I loved pitching ideas and, even more, when I sold them. I often thought of that feminist adage that has been attributed to everyone from Oprah Winfrey to Gloria Steinem to Madeleine Albright: *"Women can have it all, but not all at the same time."*

After a few years of trying and not getting pregnant, we finally consulted a specialist. We each got tested to make sure everything was in working order, and apparently it was. This brought us no relief. In some ways, a diagnosis of any kind would have led to possible treatment or at least an explanation for why nothing was happening. But with nothing medically wrong, there was nothing to fix. We were at a loss.

"You probably want a boy!" I'd cry to Joel at night.

"Hun," he'd say lovingly. "A healthy baby. A sibling for Sophie. More of us combined into one little creature. That's what I want."

"I want a boy," I'd admit in a whisper. I had grown up in a house of women. While I was close with my dad, boys were always so foreign to me. I always wished for a brother myself, so I wanted one for Sophie.

"If we did have a boy," Joel would say, "I'd want him to be left-handed."

"Your mom and Andrea are lefties."

"I know! Do you know how successful a great left-handed pitcher could be?" he'd say. "I'll tie his right arm behind his back in case he's a righty. If he could play ambidextrously, even better."

It seemed there were babies around us at all times. It was hard for Joel and me to see pregnant friends—why wasn't it happening for us? We tried to stay positive.

"Why are we stressing over having another?" Joel would ask as we'd watch Sophie draw . . . or play . . . or sneeze. "She's perfect in every way. Maybe that's why we can't get knocked up. She broke the mold."

One of my friends who had success getting pregnant recommended acupuncture, so I made an appointment. Needles were stuck all over my body while soothing candles flitted in the background. The sweet Chinese couple who ran the place would turn on a sound machine with relaxing ocean waves; the wife asked me about my diet.

"Nothing cold to eat anymore, OK? No salad. Warm food and tea. No coffee. And we'll give you herbs."

I did this for months. I enjoyed the ritual of zen-ing out twice a week for twenty minutes. We felt hopeful. I took their pills and herbal supplements and vitamins to boost my fertility. I gave up caffeine and red meat and drank protein shakes. But every month, after calculating the best time to conceive and *saving up* sex, or having sex like crazy—nothing.

Eventually I took hormones to produce more eggs, but they made me overly emotional and weepy. I went to the doctor to have her inseminate me at the exact right time of the month, but again—nothing. Joel and I realized that the change in diet and shots and doctor appointments were doing us in. Every month was an emotional roller coaster, and it had been like this *for five years*. Living with the possibility of getting pregnant every month was causing a tremendous amount of anxiety and disappointment. We kept going back to the idea that we already had a child. An amazing child who we loved and adored and who was good and kind and smart and beautiful.

Joel and I loved each other. We loved Sophie. We loved our life together. We were a family already, and that was everything. Together, we mourned the family we thought we would have . . . and by focusing on what we did have—*which was so much!*—we were able to move forward.

~

Joel was now in a teaching hospital, which meant there was never just one doctor, but one doctor being trailed by anywhere from one to four other doctors. Some were already specialists in their particular area of study, others may have been residents, but it was a continual parade of smart, ambitious, and perplexed doctors and legitimate wannabe doctors who looked at Joel's illness as a mystery they were determined to solve. I'll never forget how young these doctors were.

"It looks like they're in Halloween costumes dressed up as doctors," I said to my bestie, Jillian, who was at the hospital with me almost every day that October. She and I had met when I first moved back from New York. We grew up together working in television. We were at each other's weddings and there for the birth of each of our children. Having her with me while Joel was in the hospital was a huge comfort. "I keep expecting them to say, 'Trick or treat,'" I said.

She shushed me with a nudge. One of the doctors overheard. He rolled his eyes, but I didn't care. *Just figure out what's happening to Joel . . . and tell me that I'll be bringing him home soon.*

It was after a group of four pulmonary specialists examined him one morning that I realized what we were dealing with. One of the four, a woman whose name I must have written down somewhere, pulled me aside and gently asked, "Is your husband a man of dignity?"

By now, it was hard to keep track of which doctor did what. There were cardiologists, pulmonologists, a slew of neurologists, physical therapists. I didn't understand why a *lung doctor* was even part of Joel's team. But this gentle and well-meaning doctor had pulled me aside and asked me about Joel's dignity. I told her: "Quality of life is important to him." That was my line. That is what I told every doctor and nurse who walked into his room, whether it was to take his temperature or draw blood. Because he had MS, Joel and I had had many discussions on life and how we wanted to live it. We wanted to grow old together. We wanted to be healthy. We wanted to live fully. Quality of life, for Joel, meant that he would remain active and self-sufficient. He did not want to rely on someone else to feed him. Having just turned fifty years old, he did not want to be in diapers.

She put her hand on my elbow. "What I mean is, is he someone who wants to be perfectly capable of being independent."

I looked at her. "Yes, absolutely."

"Well," she said, "it looks that as of now, the kind of recovery we can hope for is that he may be able to hold a comb one day." I tried to breathe, but it came out as gasps as she continued. "But he wouldn't know what to do with it."

What is the proper reaction for a wife when she hears this about her once healthy husband? There was not enough air in the room for me to breathe. My mind was swirling, I felt myself go blank.

"Thank you," I managed to say. The truth is, I appreciated her clarity. I nodded my head. I understood what she was saying. I watched as she walked away. I stood in the hospital hallway by myself. I leaned against the wall, sighed heavily, and slowly let my back slide down the wall until I was seated, my legs splaying out in front of me.

I started to cry. It was the kind of cry that comes from someplace so deep inside that it felt like I was made of water. It had been over two weeks since this trauma had started. Two weeks of uncertainty. Of fear. Of confusion.

I knew that Joel wanted no part of what was happening to him. There were countless doctors, nurses, and specialists. One invasive procedure after another, all trying to establish his diagnosis. *How did he fall into a coma? What is this that is wreaking havoc on his brain and central nervous system? Will he be able to recover?*

I realized that everything was up to me now. I knew in my soul that everything I did from this point forward had to be for Joel. He no longer had a voice, so I was his voice. Sitting there in the hospital hallway, my tears nowhere close to drying up, I knew that Joel and I were connected, and this gave me strength for the many decisions I would soon have to make on his behalf.

SIX

Holding On

There's a photo I have of Joel and Sophie that makes me happy and sad at the same time. We were riding on a Hop On Hop Off tourist bus in Barcelona, Spain. In the photo they are both asleep but sitting upright in their seats, with their chins resting heavily on their chests. We had arrived the night before, but for some reason, I wasn't feeling jet-lagged. We had been exploring the city all morning. Joel and Sophie sat together on the upstairs part of the bus; I was on the lower part, studying the map and figuring out where we should get off and what sites to see. A stop was coming up, so I went upstairs to get them and found them both sound asleep. I couldn't believe it. We were in Barcelona! There was so much to take in! But here were my two travel companions, out cold.

It was hot, mid-August, and the city was crowded. The two of them were spent. Given the traveling, touring, and general tumult that comes with such a big trip, it wasn't out of the ordinary to fall asleep on a bus less than twenty-four hours after arriving. But Joel wasn't just exhausted, he was fatigued. There's a difference. He wasn't bouncing back as fast as he used to. This was apparent throughout the whole vacation.

Sophie was ten years old at the time, and it was the first and only time all of us were in Europe together. We wanted to honor Joel's wish to travel before his condition got worse. At the time, I didn't believe that the disease would progress to the point where Joel wouldn't be able to walk, but we both liked the idea of travel and taking a big family trip.

The journey we planned was a week-long cruise that went round trip from Barcelona (where we would spend several nights before the cruise), through the South of France, then on to Italy with stops in Florence and Rome before making the return to Spain. After the cruise we planned to spend some time in London visiting friends.

"Why are people talking to you in Spanish?" Sophie asked me when we were in Park Güell one afternoon.

"I think they think I'm Spanish for some reason," I said.

Joel chimed in, "You kind of look it."

"*Es posible,*" I shot back.

Joel continued. "And your high school Spanish has held up *muy bueno*!"

As a family, we were making small adjustments. As we toured the cities, I carried a heavier backpack with guidebooks, water, sunscreen, and a camera. Joel carried a small bag with our snacks, passports, and money. Joel was stoic, as always, but between the heat and all the walking, it was too much for him.

In Pompeii, a week later, we were on a morning tour of the ancient ruins. It was ninety degrees outside and the air was thick and humid. Sophie and I kept up with the group, and Joel, who had said he was fine to take the heavier backpack, lingered a bit behind.

"Hun," I said to him. "Let's switch." I handed him the lighter bag.

"No. I'm good," he said. "Just taking it all in."

I moved ahead with Sophie but kept a watchful eye on Joel. His walking was fine back then but the ground was uneven. The heat was oppressive. He had to take breaks, and he moved slowly.

"Hun," I said again a little while later. "Please." I handed him the small pack, holding out my hand for the large one.

He sighed and gave in.

"You're making a big deal out of nothing," he said. "I'm really fine. I don't like you treating me like I'm not."

"I know," I said. "I'm a pain in the ass."

But that's how the trip went. I continued to be a pain in the ass. Joel did his best but would acquiesce when I insisted on doing the heavy lifting. The symptoms of MS weren't so bad then, but he *felt* them. He didn't like being the slow guy in the back . . . or having to pack his medications and keep up that routine while we were away . . . The MS was persistent. It came on vacation with us.

Sophie, meanwhile, didn't notice the nuances of Joel's condition. Sometimes when he was just a few steps behind or needed to sit down for a minute, I'd tell her, "Daddy's OK. He just needs a break right now."

She'd ask, "Is it his MS?"

"Yup!" I'd answer. "But I think we could all use a rest anyway."

She understood. Joel's MS was simply a matter of fact. She didn't worry over it because Joel and I were accepting that this was part of our life.

When I think of Sophie in those preteen years, I remember that she was so happy and easygoing. I always say that she got her patience, kindness, and empathy from Joel. She may have his eyes and my hair, but all of her *goodness* comes from him. It's evident in the way she documented our trip. She loved making short videos explaining where we were and what we were doing.

"Hi, I'm Sophie!" she'd say into the camera. "Here we are at the Spanish Steps. It might sound like we're in Spain, but we're not! We're in Italy!" And she'd wave her arm behind her in a grand gesture to show the Spanish Steps in Rome. I love those videos; she can't even look at them now. She's mortified by what she wore, how she sounded, what she looked like. But she was adorable and chronicled our trip in a memorable way. Sometimes if I really want to annoy her, all I have to do is say *Hi, I'm Sophie!* in an affected voice for her to roll her eyes and scream, *M-o-o-o-m!*

Joel managed well for the most part, but if we had the option of finding an out-of-the-way gelato shop or art gallery, or of getting back on the ship, Joel almost always, and uncharacteristically, preferred heading back to the ship. There was a day in the South of France when Joel and Sophie didn't get off the boat, even though we had a tour booked. Sophie wasn't feeling great; all of the *exotic* foods and continuous motion of the ship and our city touring wasn't sitting well with her. Rather than encourage her to try to do the easy, air-conditioned exploration tour of Nice and Monaco, Joel quickly offered to stay behind with her.

I gave him a look. "Really, hun?"

"Yeah," he said. "I could use a day off." He kissed me and said, "But you should go."

"Yeah, Mom. Have fun. Daddy and I will be fine," Sophie said.

Them staying behind gave me pause. It was always like Joel to give up the best seat or the best piece of cake or the best *anything* for me, but I worried that maybe he wasn't feeling as good as he let on. Yet I also didn't want to miss Nice. We were in the South of France! I wanted to see it.

So I went. Alone. I ate crepes. Explored a gorgeous open-air market with some of the most beautiful flowers I have ever seen. I managed fine on my own, but I missed Joel and Sophie. I would have had a better time if we had all been together.

By the time we got to London, Joel seemed better. There wasn't quite as much schlepping. The climate was cooler. We spoke the language. We had the best time with our friends! We saw plays, went to Stonehenge, watched the changing of the guards. That trip to Europe was worth the time, effort, and expense. It was everything we had hoped it would be, even if Joel had to move at a different pace.

We were gone sixteen days. In that time, we experienced different cities and languages and adventures. We tasted new foods and learned the most basic and conversational phrases in Spanish, French, and Italian. We were active and busy; we met people from Ireland and Ohio. We had high tea and Limoncello and tapas. We traveled by plane, by boat, by train. We lived a lot of life in those sixteen days.

It was now the same amount of time that Joel had been in the ICU.

His EEGs revealed that his brain function had slowed down significantly. One of the neurologists said that Joel had paralysis from the waist down. They feared that whatever this virus was, it was attacking Joel's central nervous system. He was on a machine that helped him breathe. He was being fed by an IV. They still talked about Joel *recovering*. But to what end? The thing both Joel and I cared about the most—his quality of life—had already been severely compromised. Intellectually, I knew things were dire. But emotionally, I was still holding on.

Every day I went to the hospital. I was on the morning shift and would go directly from dropping Sophie off at school. I overlapped with Hal, who would come around lunchtime. He would stay a few hours until Joel's mother, Nancy, would come and sit with Joel in the evenings. It took a lot of coordinating. Because I was the wife, I was the only one the doctors would relay any information to. Every night, I would call Hal and Nancy with an update.

One night I could barely get the words out when I called Nancy. "It's not good," I started. I didn't bother holding back my tears. She gasped.

"The neurologist says he's paralyzed."

55

She gasped again.

"His brain activity has slowed down a lot."

"Oh no!" she cried.

"Nancy!" I shouted. "I can't keep doing this! You have to let me talk. I know it's difficult, but I have to call Hal when I hang up with you. I'm trying to relay information so you have it, but I'm the one who's doing everything and managing everyone, and I can't listen to you freaking out."

"I'm sorry," she said. I felt terrible. Joel was her son. What mother *wouldn't* react to hearing this kind of news about their child? I tried to breathe, to calm myself.

"I'm sorry, Nancy. This has been going on a long time. I just . . . I need a break," I cried. I tried to breathe as we wept together on the phone.

After a while, I said, "I miss Joel."

"I know you do, honey. So do I."

I knew people were concerned for me and Sophie, but I was in survival mode, attempting to manage everyone and everything. Still, I saw how tragic this was for Nancy and Hal. Hal, somehow, remained positive. For Nancy, seeing Joel like this was intolerable. I've come to realize that it doesn't matter if your child is five months, five years, or fifty years old. They are still your child. To see them suffer in any way, especially in a coma in the ICU of a hospital, is beyond devastating. I wanted to offer everyone my comfort; they wanted to offer me theirs. It felt overwhelming.

I got into bed that night heavy with grief. Sophie was already asleep in what was becoming her side of the bed—formerly Joel's. I thought of Joel and all that he had endured.

We were coming up on Joel's third week in the hospital. Almost twenty-one days. They say it takes twenty-one days to start or break a habit.

The habit that seemed to be taking shape was a life without Joel.

I cried myself to sleep in the same clothes I had been wearing all day.

Jillian met me at the hospital the next day. The same young doctor who looked like he was just dressing for the part a week earlier stood in front of me. Jillian had her notepad ready as she did whenever the doctors came in with news. She clutched a tissue to her nose and was seated next to Joel while I stood across from the doctor expectantly. He was extremely somber and had difficulty saying what he came in to tell me.

"So, the cultures came back . . ." He shuffled his foot.

"OK, good!" I said, hopeful.

Joel had been tested for a wide variety of viruses at the first hospital. They all came back negative. Because his symptoms persisted, many of the same tests, along with tests for different diseases and viruses, were given and repeated every few days to determine which antibodies, if any, were present in the cultures. This was the moment we had all been waiting for.

Jillian turned to face him; we both perked up. He looked around and settled his gaze at his feet.

The doctor struggled. "He, um . . . They came back positive for West Nile virus."

"Oh my God," Jillian quietly said. "Poor Joel."

She had been reading about West Nile and other viruses for weeks to try to get a sense of what was wreaking such havoc on Joel. She would then filter the information to me so that I could have an educated conversation with the doctors whenever there was something new to discuss.

Most people infected with West Nile virus do not develop symptoms. With a mild infection, a person may experience sore throat, body aches, and fatigue. At its most severe, the virus can cause inflammation of the brain and spinal cord, coma, and paralysis.

"OK. So what does that mean exactly?" I asked. I was calm, somehow, direct.

Once again, a doctor couldn't look at me. I thought he was about to cry. I could see how hard he was trying to maintain composure. It seemed he drew the shortest stick in the group meeting that day, and he was the one who, reluctantly, had to deliver the news.

I looked at Jillian, who was facing Joel and crying quietly into a tissue. She ran her fingers through his hair.

I looked at the doctor and said again, "OK. So now we know it's West Nile. What happens next?"

A part of me thought there'd be an antidote. A fix. Something that would make Joel all better. But another part of me, the part that was the most scared, knew there was no such thing.

The doctor stayed silent.

"OK," I tried again. "Let's say this was happening to someone you loved. What would you do? How would you move forward?"

He seemed to be working very hard on his answer.

Finally, he said, "Well, if this were one of my parents, I would consider that they both lived long lives. Lived nice lives. I would understand if the decision was made to . . . to . . . um . . ."

He didn't finish his sentence. He didn't need to. Because of my unexpected and recent education with viruses, I knew that even the most benign ones, like a common cold or flu, simply need to run their course. West Nile virus had run its course on my husband.

Earlier in the week, there was talk of moving Joel to a rehab facility. This would require a *PEG and trach*, which was a way to keep him alive. The peg was actually a hole they would make in his stomach and attach a feeding tube through. The trach stood for tracheostomy—a hole that would go through his throat so he could be permanently attached to a breathing machine. Currently, and for weeks, he had a breathing tube down his throat. The doctors all felt that the breathing tube was becoming dangerous this many days in, that an infection could develop and threaten the patient's well-being.

What well-being? I thought.

Joel was right there in front of me. His hair was longer. His beard was full. He was warm to the touch, and I could feel his heart beating through the thin hospital gown. The whir of machines keeping him stable provided a soundtrack I could not get out of my head for close to a year. I held his limp hand and put it on my cheek and maneuvered between the ubiquitous tubes and put my other hand on his face.

I felt him holding on, waiting for me to let him go.

SEVEN

Decisions

O nce we all understood that Joel had West Nile virus, we scheduled a family meeting with a hospital social worker and the doctor who admitted Joel—the same one who nonchalantly told me he was in a coma. As the head of the neurological ICU, she was there to answer our questions. She walked in flustered and ill prepared. "I'm sorry, I wasn't even aware we were having a meeting this morning. What would you like to know?" was how she began. She seemed impatient, almost defensive, as if she thought we might blame her for some kind of medical failure on the part of the hospital and/ or her staff.

She dealt with medical trauma every single day. My family was in emotional trauma, but her attitude made it clear: she didn't know how to manage the care *we* needed.

We understood that Joel was paralyzed and had brain damage because West Nile virus had wreaked havoc on his central nervous system. His multiple sclerosis had made him susceptible to West Nile. His MS meds had stopped working, and the steroid infusion treatment he was on to boost his system made him immunocompromised. Which is why he wasn't allowed to leave the house while they were being administered. The steroids made him susceptible to any kind of infection or cold. His body would not be able to fight back.

Nothing would make my husband better.

I thought about our backyard. It was one of Joel's happy places. He loved tending to our rose bushes and tomatoes. He loved trimming the shrubs around the pool. He would roll around the wheelbarrow we got him one Father's Day and fill it with lemons from our prolific citrus tree. But at the time of the infusions, all he would do outside is nap. Putter around. He knew better than to do his usual gardening, nor did he have the capacity to.

West Nile virus is commonly transmitted via mosquito, and being in our backyard proved lethal. We just didn't know it at the time.

It took weeks for Joel to become symptomatic. Starting with his high fever all those weeks earlier.

Unbeknownst to me, while Joel was in the hospital, my neighbors in our little cul-de-sac had been furiously calling and emailing our councilman and the department of public health. That summer in Los Angeles, talk of West Nile virus was everywhere. Thirteen people contracted it, and one person had died. There were mosquito warning flyers up in summer camps, doctors' offices, and even some supermarkets. In one of the first emails I had Greg send out to our friends, he mentioned that Joel had been tested for a variety of illnesses, one of them being West Nile virus. This was all my neighbors needed to hear. They all adored Joel and were concerned for our family. Our dog-loving neighbor, Roxanne, in particular, bonded with Joel every time he was out front, cutting back our abundance of roses. She would be doing the same in her front yard just a few houses down.

We were all upset about the house next door to us. It had been purchased by a developer months earlier, and construction turning it into a McMansion had not yet started. The house had fallen into gross disrepair with an overgrown lawn and backyard swimming pool that had been half drained and became more like a swamp. We all believed that this pool must have been where the infected mosquito came from. It seemed quite apparent. But because one can't confirm or track the flight pattern of a mosquito, we were unable to prove any wrongdoing or press charges of any kind.

In the meeting, I asked the doctor, "Is the ventilator what's keeping Joel alive?"

Her eyes met mine and, realizing my need for her to state the obvious, she said, "If we took away the machine, it's unlikely your husband would be able to breathe on his own."

"And if he can't breathe on his own, he would . . . ?" I let my voice trail. I didn't want to say the word *die*.

She nodded and simply said, "That's right."

Hal chimed in, "So, would you consider the ventilator to be life support?"

The doctor didn't hesitate. "Yes," she said. "That's exactly what it is."

We all looked at each other, stunned. In the throes of all the medical confusion and trying to figure out what was happening to him and why, none of us had fully realized it. Joel had been on a breathing machine before we left the first hospital. They used it to support his breathing, but at the time he was still capable of breathing on his own. With his body breaking down with something new every day, the machine was now supporting his life. Just like asking if he was in a coma, if Hal hadn't asked that question, we wouldn't have known.

Joel has brain damage.

Joel is paralyzed.

Joel is on life support.

It was clear to me that I had a decision to make about my husband. We left that meeting, and I took the rest of the day to process everything. This was my decision to make and mine alone. I wanted Joel's suffering to end. I did not have the stamina to consider how I could have a life without him. It seemed so impossible. *Who will I laugh with?*

Who will explain things to me the way that Joel does? Who will parent Sophie with me? Who will love me so unconditionally? Who will I spend my life with?

All I wanted was for Joel to overcome this. The MS. The West Nile. His suffering. In many ways, death was the only option, and it was time. I knew with absolute certainty this is what Joel would want. He would be relieved.

"Finally!" he would have said, laughing. "Seriously, hun. What took you so long?"

Now it was a matter of timing. If I had said to the doctor that morning, "Turn off the life support today," she would have.

But it was my birthday. I did not want my husband to die on my birthday.

A few days later, it would be Halloween. Sophie was excited. She had her Snow White costume and plans with friends. I wanted her to have one night of fun before our world came crashing down.

So I chose the day after Halloween, as if it would make a difference, to end his life.

Hal, meanwhile, did not agree with my decision. He was angry and wanted answers. The following morning, he and I met with the other head doctor of the neurological ICU. This doctor made the first doctor we spoke with seem relaxed and casual. He spoke medically, with even less bedside manner. Hal was insistent. He thought they needed to try everything, explore all options, even though they already had been, for weeks.

"I don't agree with Melissa's decision! There has to be something you can do!" Hal challenged.

"There is no treatment for these viruses," the doctor said.

"Well, I don't want him paralyzed," Hal said. It was as if he was realizing for the first time just how dire the circumstances were.

"But he already is," said the doctor. Hal was turning paler by the second.

"Sometimes they wake." The doctor continued, "It's not pretty."

"How can you say that to me? Do you have a son? Or a child? Do you?" Hal demanded to know. "Do you?"

I imagined a doctor saying something like this to Joel and me. *What if this were Sophie? What if it were my parents the doctor was talking to?*

The doctor shook his head. He looked Hal directly in his eyes.

"You do not want your son to wake up from this," he said.

"But I do!" Hal cried.

"You don't. If your son were to wake up," the doctor said, "it would be a fate worse than death."

Hal sat there, deflated and defeated. It took some time for us both to compose ourselves. We were sitting in the ICU. Business went on as usual. Nurses and doctors popping in and out with medications and gurneys and IV bags. There was sickness all around us. We both needed air.

Before we left the hospital, one of the nurses came to me in tears.

"I just want to tell you," she said, "letting him go is the most loving thing you could do for your husband. You're doing the right thing. I promise."

I drove Hal home that day. Together we called Nancy from the car. She had been in the family meeting the day before, and even though she knew my decision, she was thinking that perhaps rehab was a good place for Joel. We could keep up the same visiting schedule, she had suggested; *miracles can happen.*

I did not want to be in this position. Of convincing Joel's parents of the "right thing" to do on behalf of their son. But I was. We hadn't heard Joel's voice for weeks, but my sister reminded me of the emails he had sent his doctors when we got home from Mexico, each one a cry for help. I decided to share them with Joel's family. This one in particular impacted them:

Dr. K—My wife and I are very concerned. My legs continue to weaken and I feel I'm deteriorating rapidly. I can barely feel my feet and my balance has become a significant issue. I've also been experiencing numbness from the waist down that I never had before. Every day has become challenging. I'm experiencing severe leg, foot, and core problems and my life is being impacted in ways that are frightening.

We all knew that Joel had been suffering, but hearing it, seeing it spelled out in his own words, eliminated any doubts.

In many ways I was relieved. I was eerily calm. Where nothing but confusion existed for weeks, things were now crystal clear. I was ending Joel's life.

I now had to tell Sophie.

EIGHT

The End

I t was dark outside, and the conversation took place in our kitchen. Sophie and I agree on those details.

Sophie thinks the conversation started when she asked me a question about Joel to which I answered, "We are taking him off of life support on Friday."

I believe that I started it by saying something like, "I need to tell you what's going on with Daddy."

My tone was casual. We also agree on this. I didn't want Sophie to see that I was bereft, and I didn't want to be overly dramatic. The situation in itself was dramatic. I didn't want to start with, *Soph, we need to talk about something serious*. Even to our thirteen-year-old, that was stating the obvious. Nor did I want it to feel light or unimportant. If there was a healthy or "correct" way to tell your child that her father was dying, I wasn't aware of it.

"You know Daddy's in a coma." Sophie nodded yes. "And it's very sad because the doctors think that if he ever woke up, he wouldn't be the daddy we know. He wouldn't know me, he wouldn't know our house. He wouldn't even know you." That's when my voice started to crack. I wanted to grab her and hold her and let her cry and scream in my arms. But she was stoic, just like her dad; so I tried to be, too.

"Would he be in a wheelchair?" she asked.

"Yes, he would," I said. "But he wouldn't be able to push it."

"So who would?" she asked. "Us?"

"I don't think Daddy would like either of us having to take care of him that way."

She nodded.

"Someone else would have to," I said. "Like a nurse. Someone else would have to do everything for him. He wouldn't be able to eat on his own, or brush his teeth, or go to the bathroom."

She was taking it all in, trying to comprehend these impossible words I was saying.

Joel was not a "weekend" kind of father. He was hands-on. He and Sophie were deeply connected. He was in awe of her kindness, her intelligence, her talent. I could go on. We were both besotted with her.

"So would we put a ramp in the house?"

This is when I started to cry. I tried to maintain my composure, which wasn't difficult as I was totally numb. I couldn't believe I was having this conversation with our child. I couldn't believe my husband was the person I was talking about. Her father. Our family.

"The thing is, I don't think Daddy will be coming home."

In an instant, I saw something in her face change. It was as if she went from the innocence and bliss of childhood to the shattering realities of adulthood. Tears welled up behind her eyes.

I want to say that I held her and that we cried and wailed together. It's possible that we did. Neither of us remembers.

Eventually I told her the plan for the next few days.

"So I know Halloween is in a few days. You can still go out with your friends and dress up. But the next day, in the morning, we're going to say goodbye to Daddy."

"Will I go to school that day?" she asked. Which killed me in a way I can't explain. She was a rule follower, a good person, like Joel.

"No, Smoosh. You won't have to go to school that day or even the following week. We'll see how you're doing after that. You have the week off for Thanksgiving coming up, too, and we'll just take it day by day. Give you the time you need, OK? Your teachers and everyone, they understand."

When Joel was first moved downtown, I set up a meeting with the on-site therapist at Sophie's middle school. She was new that year; she was young, and very kind. I wanted her to know what was going on so that if Sophie needed a quiet space to retreat to during the day or simply someone to talk to—someone other than me—about what was going on, she'd be able to. The therapist also acted as liaison with Sophie's teachers, all of whom were compassionate and devastated by what was happening at home with one of their favorite students. They checked in with me frequently and were on the growing list of people who were getting the email updates.

Sophie accepted what I told her. Just seeing Joel in the hospital for those three weeks—which sometimes seems like three years, and alternatively, three minutes—was scary for her. She seemed to understand that there was no life left for Joel to live. At some point that night, we got into my bed and snuggled. Together we cried.

There was a game show that Joel and Sophie liked to watch together when she was younger. For the life of me, I could not understand how the show worked. It had to do with suitcases containing money, a hidden banker, and contestants guessing which suitcase had the most money in it, which could potentially be their prize. At 7:30 p.m., after a bath and before books, they'd watch a half an hour of TV. I can still hear them shouting, *Wheel! Of! Fortune!* Or *doot-doot-doing* to the theme song of *The Simpsons*. I didn't have to be in the same room to hear Sophie's giggles or know that Joel was smiling as they sat smushed together on the couch. He loved this time with her, and I loved that they had their routines.

Sometimes as they were watching their show, I would walk through the room and mutter, "I really don't get it."

"Hun," Joel would say with a laugh, "it's so simple. There are twenty-six suitcases, and they're trying to guess which one has the most money in it. Then the banker will make an offer that could be more or less than what's in the suitcase. That's the risk of the game!"

"But who's the banker?" I'd want to know.

"It doesn't matter who the banker is!" Joel would say, exasperated.

"Just watch and you'll get it, Mom! It's not that hard," my third grader would say as she and Joel shared an eye roll.

But I never got it.

For me, easy was sometimes difficult. Without Joel, I worried how I would understand anything.

My heart broke for Sophie more than it did for myself. *What must she be feeling?* At that point in time, the only experience she had with death was our beloved cat, Puddin'. Losing a pet does not prepare a child for the death of a parent. Her four sets of grandparents were all alive and well.

It's unnatural for a child to lose a parent before her grandparents.

Just as it's unthinkable that a parent outlives their child, this was out of order. It made no sense.

The fact that Hal had lost his own father at the same age as Sophie was, thirteen, seemed particularly cruel that he was now, at seventy-three, about to also lose his son.

Elisabeth, too, had lost her mother as a young girl of ten years old.

My mother lost her father at seventeen.

The grandparents provided me with some solace that although this loss seemed unbearable, it was survivable. While Sophie was aware of these facts, losing Joel was no comparison. This loss was hers.

I continued to go to the hospital every day that week. I called a select group of friends to come and say their goodbyes. I thought of who Joel would want to see and who he wouldn't mind seeing him so compromised. I had acclimated to seeing him nonresponsive with tubes everywhere. But our friends weren't. They all thought of Joel as energetic and alive. Even with my warning that it wouldn't be easy to see him like this, it was shocking for almost everyone who came by.

With so many visitors during the preceding days and weeks, I had been growing accustomed to seeing grown men cry, but still, it was crushing every time.

One friend cried so hard he left puddles at his feet.

Another friend went to say goodbye at a time I wasn't there. He called to tell me about it and had to call me back three times. He was sobbing so hard each time he called that he couldn't get his words out.

By then I had cried so much that I thought I would run out of tears.

On Halloween, I helped Sophie get ready, and then dropped her at her friend's house with her plastic pumpkin bucket to collect candy in. She told me that she was excited to go trick or treating with her friends even though she knew she'd be saying goodbye to her dad the next day. But an hour after I dropped her off, I got a call to come pick her up.

When she got in the car, I said, "I'm sorry, Smoosh. I know it's a rough night."

She was visibly upset. "It's my hair!" she cried. "It was supposed to be curled under like Snow White, but it was taking forever and everyone was waiting to leave so we couldn't finish it. It's not how I wanted tonight to go!"

I nodded.

"I don't know why I even bothered going out." She fished around her plastic pumpkin candy bucket. "I don't even like the candy I got!"

She cried and was frustrated and quiet on the short ride home. I didn't know how to comfort her, but I was fairly certain her tears were over something much more significant than hair and candy.

There were eleven of us surrounding Joel in his hospital bed the next morning. Our immediate family, Sophie and I, and Rabbi Hannah. He was still being kept alive when Rabbi Hannah said the kaddish, the Jewish prayer for mourning. There was sobbing, there was shock; the grief in the room was palpable. It was loud. It was ugly. It was painful.

When the kaddish was over, each family member took some private time with Joel. Afterward, they all wanted to leave the hospital. I understood. This was the saddest thing I had ever experienced. They wanted to get away from it. Sophie, too, decided to leave with her grandparents. I would meet her back at our house in a few hours.

I was left alone with Joel. At this point, he was still on life support. The nurses and doctors were giving us our privacy. I am not the kind of person who wears a lot of makeup, but I had some on that day. I even wore my long hair down. I wanted to look pretty. I wanted Joel to remember me that way. I had the thought, *He is dying young. What if he doesn't recognize me when I see him again? I could be old and wrinkly, but he'll still be young and handsome.*

I remember feeling anxious when Rabbi Hannah knocked on the door.

"You're sure you're OK?" she asked.

"I'm just staying to say goodbye," I told her.

"I'm happy to stay with you," she said.

It was a Friday. A busy day for rabbis, the start of the Sabbath.

"I'm really OK," I assured her. "My best friend is coming to pick me up."

I had arranged with Jillian to bring me home from the hospital that day. She texted that she was downstairs and said I should take my time.

"Thank you for everything," I told the rabbi.

We hugged goodbye and she left.

That's when I started to really cry. *My poor Joel!* He lay there in front of me, lifeless but alive. The doctors had warned me that turning off the machines didn't necessarily mean immediate death.

"He could hold on for hours," one said. "Sometimes it takes days. But with him, it will probably be quick."

They assured me that Joel would feel no pain. For weeks he had been prodded and tested and observed. The doctors and nurses had been keeping him comfortable the whole time. I believed that death would finally provide Joel with the relief he deserved.

I was still afraid of all the wires he was connected to. It was still hard to get as close to him as I would have liked. I wanted to lie down next to him—him on his back, me on my side wrapped around him. I couldn't. These entire three weeks, I could not get close to my husband. I could not feel him respond to my touch. I could not hear his laugh.

His suffering would be over; this I knew. This was my mantra, *no more suffering . . . no more suffering.* This is the thought that gave me the strength to say goodbye. I started at the base of the bed where his feet stuck out of the light blanket.

I kissed the top of each foot.

"I love you," I whispered to him, squeezing each one of his long toes. "Finger toes" we would call them.

I moved up to his hands, careful not to disrupt the IVs, as silly as that now seems.

"Hun," I said, kissing his fingers. "You." Another kiss. "You." Another kiss. *"You."*

"I love you, hun," I cried into his palms. *"You!"*

I now held his limp hand up to my face, whispering, "No matter what occurs . . ." because I *would* find him. I would. This made me smile through my tears.

I moved up to his face. His eyes were closed as they had been. He had a feeding tube in his mouth, the same one that had been there for weeks. I stroked his now thick beard.

"It's OK, hun. You're going to be OK." I reached over everything, the wires and equipment, and kissed his head. "It's OK," I kept saying.

"You're going to be free. You're going to be free. You'll feel so much better. You will."

A thought then occurred to me. I wanted Joel to know something that in hindsight I believe he already knew. With my mouth against his forehead, I told him, "Sophie and I will be OK. I'll take care of her, hun. We will be OK."

If I thought of Sophie at all, everything inside me spilled out through gasps and sobs and tears. *How will I be able to give her a life without her father? How will I be able to do anything without Joel by my side? How will I be strong enough to raise her alone?*

But I had the sense that Joel trusted we would be OK. I didn't think he would be able to die if he had a shred of doubt about the two of us managing without him. I had a feeling that I could move forward because his love for us would give me the strength to. I held his head with both of my hands. I kissed his eyes. I took a deep breath.

I called in the doctor who was turning off life support. We had never met as his role was specific to end-of-life needs. I heard him inhale when he saw me. He looked at Joel's chart and then back at me. He shook his head and said, "I'm so sorry."

I would see the same expression from many people, but I didn't realize why at the time. I would understand it much better in the weeks and months to come. It was because both Joel and I were too young for this.

The doctor sat down next to Joel and the machine that was keeping him alive. He looked at me. I nodded as I clutched a tissue to my nose and sobbed quietly.

"I'm going to turn off the ventilator. There may be some residual noise from him, but maybe not. He won't feel any pain or discomfort." He looked at me. "Are you ready?"

Again, I nodded yes.

"OK." He did something with the machine, and suddenly the room got quiet. I didn't realize how the machine had created a white noise environment all those weeks.

He took Joel's pulse and looked at me. At the most, a minute had passed.

"He's gone." He said it kindly. "I'm sorry for your loss."

It was the first time I ever heard those words. It was stunning. I couldn't connect the dots that *my loss* was Joel.

He then called the time of death. A moment later, a nurse came in and started unplugging everything. It was bizarre. I could have told them that I needed more time, that I wanted a minute with my husband, but the truth is, I wanted to leave. I could not stand to be there with Joel when he was already gone. I suspected that he had been gone days earlier but was holding on to give everyone a chance to say goodbye. That would have been so like him, putting everyone else first.

It would drive me crazy. If we were going to the theater or to a restaurant, Joel was the guy who held the door open for everyone when all I wanted to do was get inside and get the best seat.

I texted Jillian, said I was on my way down.

It was so strange leaving the ICU. I had been there every day for the past few weeks. It was a round room with a hub in the center for the doctors and interns. There was a nurses' station and a break room. There were sick patients all around the perimeter. It smelled sterile. I did not want to say goodbye to anyone, even the nurses whom I got to know fairly well and the interns who worked so hard to understand what the cause of Joel's illness had been. I just wanted to get out of there and never, ever go back.

As I waited for the elevator, I put on my sunglasses. I continued to cry. I could not comprehend what was happening. *My husband just died.*

I saw people on their phones; friends were laughing and making plans for the weekend. People were getting on and off the elevator. *My husband just died.*

As I walked through the hospital lobby and outside its doors, people were driving their cars and looking for parking. Someone was eating a sandwich.

How could they? Didn't they know? *My husband just died.*

I saw Jillian's car. I saw her waiting for me. The sun felt warm on my face. I felt a sense of urgency. I wanted to run! I did not want to look back. I wanted to get home to Sophie.

It was over.

I wanted to tell Joel that I would find him . . .

But as I opened the car door, it didn't feel like I had left Joel alone inside the hospital.

It felt like he had left with me.

I was not going to let him go.

NINE

Doing Clooney

There's a mountain trail near my house that I've been hiking for about twenty-five years, even before I lived so close to it. It's a little over three miles long and there are a few different entry points. The trail is actually a wide path that is paved part of the way, then becomes a dirt footpath, and eventually leads you into a residential neighborhood, which happens to be where George Clooney lives when he's in Los Angeles. Because of this, my friends and I call it the Clooney hike.

There have been times in my life where I do Clooney every day, and other times when there are weeks in between. In the beginning, when Joel and I lived in my Hollywood apartment, my friend Jennie would pick me up on Saturday mornings, and we'd drive over Laurel Canyon to do Clooney. Jennie has since moved back to Chicago, and I've had a variety of walking partners over the years. And quite often, I do Clooney on my own.

You are hit with a pretty steep incline at the onset. I have a no-talking rule when starting the climb because even after so many years of schlepping up this side of the hill, I still can't catch my breath for at least the first ten minutes, let alone carry on a conversation. You zig-zag up the mountain for about another twenty minutes after that. It's rigorous, but the abundance of wildflowers and eucalyptus trees makes up for it. By the halfway point, there's a reprieve, and a short part of the trail becomes flat with spectacular views of the valley, Mulholland Drive, and snowcapped mountains in the distance. Eventually, you realize that you're walking downhill. The neighborhood appears just beyond the bend. Soon you're passing George's house, and sure enough, you've completed the loop, gotten some fresh air, and moved your body in a way that is considered exercise.

In those early days of losing Joel, my life became that hike. I kept expecting to be able to catch my breath. I kept thinking that things might get easier or at least slow down. I was waiting for the reprieve. But things weren't easy for a long time. I just kept climbing uphill. Conversations were difficult. Catching my breath, impossible. I wanted to stop hiking, stop climbing, but my every day became the climb. It was months before I could breathe again.

I was sitting at our yellow-painted dining table. It was the night Joel died. My neighbor Roxanne was leaving to pick up my dad and Elisabeth from the airport. Jillian had stayed with me since leaving the hospital. Sophie was asleep in my room.

"I'm worried about Joel," I said to Roxanne as she was heading out the door. "I'm afraid he's cold. I'm afraid he doesn't know what's happening to him."

I saw Roxanne and Jillian exchange a look.

"I think Joel's OK, honey," Roxanne said. "I don't think he's cold."

"I'm worried," I kept saying. "He's better when we're together. I think he's confused without me there."

I didn't know where *there* was. But I believed what I was saying. I believed that Joel was lost that night. That he was confused and didn't know where to go. People talk about seeing a white light when you die. That you travel through a tunnel, toward the light, and that family and friends who have passed are there to meet you. But with the exception of his grandmothers, who had died years and years earlier, there was no one "close" to help show him the way. No contemporaries, no one who had a first degree of separation. This thought had me reeling.

"He doesn't know what to do," I cried. "He doesn't know what's happening to him."

Jillian offered her comfort, too. "I think Joel's OK," she kept saying. "I don't think you need to worry."

But worry became my new normal.

Earlier that day, when I got home from the hospital, I held Sophie, and we cried.

"I really believe this, Smoosh," I said to her. "I don't think that Daddy would have let go if he didn't think we'd be OK on our own."

"I think so, too," she said. Whether or not my thirteen-year-old really agreed with me, I wasn't sure. But she was following my lead. I wanted to comfort her more than anything.

"We're going to be OK," I cried to her. "We'll be OK."

I was convincing myself of this, too. It was just the two of us now. I felt the weight of that responsibility immediately. I was mad at Joel for leaving us, but I was happy that he was no longer suffering. I could not get the thought of him in the hospital out of my mind. I kept trying to remember him from our life together, but *I couldn't get out of the hospital.*

I tried to picture him in the mail room of Atlantic. *I saw him in his hospital gown.*

I tried to remember us breaking the glass at our wedding. *I saw the tube taped down around his mouth.*

I tried to remember him laughing, elated, telling me, "She's got so much hair!" as Sophie was being born, but *I only heard the machines that were keeping him alive.*

If I couldn't have Joel with me, physically, I at least wanted my memories. They didn't exist. They couldn't. I tried to breathe, but my lungs could find no air. So I tried not to move, for fear I myself would die, too. I tried to make sense of things. I couldn't. It wasn't just that my heart was broken, my soul was shattered. All of the bones had left my body. There was nothing holding me up.

Somewhere along the line, Joel and I had decided we wanted to be cremated when we died. But a few months earlier, out of the blue when we were both getting dressed for the day, Joel said to me, "Maybe we should be buried when we die. Recycled back into the earth."

I shook my head dismissively. "Nope!" I said. "I don't want to feel guilty for not visiting you in a cemetery. And I wouldn't want you to feel guilty for not visiting me, either."

Joel thought about it for a second, then shrugged. "OK."

It was a fleeting and ridiculous conversation. But now I felt guilty. I wanted Joel cremated so I could keep him close, literally keep him next to me. I still carry some of his ashes in my yoga bag.

I wanted to be alone, but with people. I wanted to gather my thoughts, but not have a thought in my head. I wanted to come to terms with this impossible new reality, but I didn't want to think about any of it.

Our dogs were also grieving. They had been waiting weeks for Joel to come home. They were anxious and made me cry every time I walked through the door. They expected him. They wanted him.

While Joel was still in the hospital, I had gone into a holistic pet store and burst into tears. The woman who worked there came out from around the counter and held me.

"It's OK to cry." She asked, "Is your fur family sick?"

I collected myself and told this woman I had never met before, "My dogs are grieving because my husband is in a coma and they haven't seen him in weeks. They miss him."

It all poured out of me. "He had a fever. I thought he was contagious so the first night he was in the hospital, I went home and washed all of his clothes, and our sheets and towels. I didn't want us to catch whatever it was he had. But now nothing even smells like him anymore, and the dogs don't understand what's happening."

As I continued crying, she went around the store, her hand on her heart, listening empathically, shaking her head, gasping, stopping to ask, "How many dogs do you have, sweetie?"

"Two," I cried.

"How big are they?"

"A big one, like a husky. Sixtyish pounds. And a small, neurotic one. Twenty-five pounds."

The woman went shelf to shelf, read labels, and gathered potions and ointments.

By the time I finished—". . . and he won't be coming home because he's been on life support, and we're turning it all off on Friday"—she was at the register ringing up antianxiety oils and pills and treatments. She wiped tears from her face as she collected everything and put it in a bag.

"Please come back and tell me how they're doing," she said. She hugged me again. "I will pray for you and your husband."

I took her prayers along with the doggy meds and left.

Sophie and I needed to pick out the clothes we would wear for the small memorial service at Hal and Rita's. That meant getting dressed. Looking presentable. *What does one wear to her husband's memorial?*

My friend Mimi had kindly arranged for Sophie and me to get our hair done. I don't know how I was able to leave the house, let alone drive somewhere, but I did. When we got to the hair salon, they didn't have our reservation. They were busy and asked if we could come back tomorrow. I started to lose it. "No, we can't come back tomorrow, because today is my husband's memorial. He died!" I screamed, apparently. "My husband died and my daughter and I need to get our hair done. Today!"

Sophie was mortified.

At the small family-only memorial, I sat in the backyard of my in-laws' house, holding hands with my daughter as Rabbi Hannah eulogized Joel. It was the same spot on the deck where sixteen years earlier, Joel and I had said, "I do."

I had been a reluctant bride all those years ago. It seemed everyone was divorced. My parents, Joel's parents, Joel . . . I never fantasized about my wedding day. I loved Joel and wanted to build a life with him, and while I would have been happy to elope, he convinced me to have a small wedding.

"Come on, hun. I want the people we care about to see how much I love you. Marry me."

How could I resist?

We said our "I dos" under the chuppah in Hal and Rita's backyard with beautiful and expansive views of the valley. The sixty people who attended tell me it was one of the best weddings they have ever been to. It wasn't lavish or over-the-top; it was intimate and full of love.

Our first dance as husband and wife was to the Lemonheads song "Into Your Arms."

But before that, Joel cued up the James Taylor song "How Sweet It Is" to start playing right after we kissed and stepped on a wine glass and everyone yelled, "Mazel tov!" In a Jewish wedding, breaking the glass symbolizes the ancient destruction of the temple in Jerusalem. As Jews, we remember that, even during moments of extreme joy, we should be mindful of suffering.

We would have never guessed how prophetic this tradition was for us.

The view was the same, but the landscape had changed entirely. Sixteen years earlier, Joel and I looked out and envisioned our future together; now I couldn't imagine a future without him.

Ellie, the arbiter of all things Jewish in my life, suggested that I hold shiva. My dad and Elisabeth encouraged me to do the same. Shiva is a Jewish ritual—a period of mourning where people come together to remember and celebrate the person who has just died. So many people had been reaching out, asking about a service or memorial, so shiva made sense to me. Ellie and my family of friends, along with Elisabeth, arranged everything, and shiva took place at our house a couple of days later.

I wore a dress that first day of shiva; I don't recall wearing shoes. I sent an email, encouraging Sophie's friends to attend. I tried to make a movie montage of Joel, something I had started for his fiftieth birthday a few months earlier but had never finished. I wanted to play it on a loop but our reliable computer crashed suddenly. I think Joel was telling me, *Don't worry about the movie, hun. You've got enough to do.* So I let that go.

My house was full of people. People whom Joel and I loved. People who we didn't see often enough. It was like a party. My funky yellow dining table was covered with food, along with every surface in my kitchen. There was music playing, thanks to Joel's best friend, Greg, who took over what would typically have been Joel's responsibility.

Ellie passed me with a platter of sandwiches. "You'll have food for days!"

Mimi walked around with a trash bag, picking up after people. "Don't worry," she said. "We're cleaning as we go."

Elisabeth gave me a hug. "You just relax, Melissa." And she moved on to put some flowers someone brought into a vase.

But I was relaxed, and I wasn't worried. Sophie was running through the house with her friends. Some of her teachers were there. Her soccer coach from years ago, her preschool babysitter, family and friends I hadn't seen in years.

But people seemed to steer clear of me. Not too many approached. I saw some of Joel's friends from the softball team he played on when we first got together. I was excited to see them. *It had been so long!* But none of them looked at me. I finally went up to them.

"You guys!" Two of them had tears in their eyes but tried to smile. One of them hugged me. "I'm so sorry," he said. "We're all going to miss him."

I realized that he was crying. I looked around. My house was packed. There were so many familiar faces! People from yoga, a family we knew from our neighborhood who we ran into on Joel's birthday trip to Mexico, our neighbors. It made me so happy to see everyone.

But I kept looking for the one face that wasn't there.

Joel's.

And then I remembered. Joel wouldn't be walking out of the kitchen with a plate full of food. He wasn't going to be coming in from the backyard having just gone for a swim. He wouldn't be walking through the front door with the dogs from a walk.

He would never be coming home.

I hate the word *dead*. It's so cold and final. I rarely use it. Joel is gone, Joel died, but I won't say *he is dead*. It's too shocking, too painful.

But that is why people are filling up my house.

That is why people are looking at me with pity.

That is why people are scared of me.

My husband died.

It hit me hard. My heart was pounding. The room started to spin. I didn't want to see these people anymore. I started to heave, trying to breathe, but again there wasn't enough air in the room.

I went into my bedroom and closed the door. I got under the covers in all of my clothes, and the weight of the world came with me.

I miss you, hun.

Where are you?

When will I see you again?

I let myself cry, and after a while, I was able to steady my breath. I clung to Joel's pillow and liked that it felt wet from my tears. It was proof that this was real. I needed proof because it was all too hard to believe.

My body relaxed. I thought of Joel, I tried to see him smiling and laughing, but all I could do was see him in the hospital. He was tired. So tired. He was suffering. I ended his suffering. Now mine was beginning. *Who will end mine?*

I felt deflated and not just alone, but lonely. My house was full of people—people who would all be leaving. Going back to their own homes with their spouses. They'd share their disbelief that Joel had died.

He was young. He had more life to live. It's so sad!

They'd express their concern for *poor Melissa* . . . and *poor Sophie.*

My house was full of love and sadness. I had never seen so many people under my roof.

None of them knew what I knew. That Joel was in bad shape long before he went to the hospital. They didn't know how anxious Joel felt going to bed at night because waking up every day he was met with uncertainty over how he would be feeling. *Would he be able to get out of bed? Would he be able to concentrate at work? Would he be able to safely get Sophie to school?* These are the thoughts that kept him awake at night.

"I won't use it!" Joel said angrily when I told him I had applied for a disabled parking placard for him earlier that year.

"But you need it! There's no shame in it."

"I can still walk," he said. "You act like I'm incapacitated."

"Not at all! But if you have this disease, let's take advantage of the perks. Closer parking, especially living in LA, is a perk!"

Joel didn't want to give in. Not just to me and the argument that I was making, but to the MS. Early that summer, we had gone to a concert at the Greek Theatre. It's a beautiful outdoor venue that feels uniquely Los Angeles. It is tucked away in the mountains in an "Old Hollywood" neighborhood. Parking was a pain in the ass because of traffic, plus it was ridiculously expensive. For years we would park about a mile away in the hilly neighborhood that surrounds the Greek and walk up the residential streets to get to the theater and back.

When we were leaving the concert that night, after hours of standing and sitting and moving, the walk back to the car was too much for Joel to manage. What normally took twenty minutes took over an hour. We had to stop frequently so Joel could rest. In what seemed like an everyday occurrence, Joel's legs becoming more like stilts and nearly impossible to bend made the walk that much more difficult. By the time we were in the thick of the neighborhood, Joel sat on someone's front lawn, completely spent.

"I hate this," he said. "I'm sorry."

I kissed him. "Don't worry. I need this. I didn't exercise today!" I said. I then trotted up the street a few more blocks to where our car was parked. I tried to make light of the situation, but I knew it was killing him. Joel felt emasculated.

"What kind of husband am I if I can't even walk my wife to our car?" he asked, getting into the car.

"The best kind," I told him. I reached over and squeezed his hand. It offered him no reassurance. He felt completely defeated, but I felt strongly that if we could keep things "normal" and continue to do the things we loved, it might help Joel feel better. Even if it was something as mundane as convenient parking.

It didn't occur to me as we drove home that night, my mind racing, worrying about my husband and his health, worrying about our life and our future together, that it would be a life without him in it.

"Sissy?"

I opened my eyes and pulled down the covers to find my sister.

"Are you OK?" Holly asked. "Shiva is still going on."

But I wasn't ready to talk. I wanted to stay in the cocoon of my bed. It was warm and comfortable. Joel was there with me. I felt him.

"I'm just going to stay here," I told Holly. "Maybe forever."

"You can do that," she said. "But Sophie is looking for you."

Sophie!

I jumped up just as she appeared in the doorway.

"Mom?" she said.

There was my girl. My beautiful girl with her thick brown hair and her daddy's green eyes. They were full of tears. I lifted back the covers.

"Come." Sophie ran into bed and got under the covers with me. Like me, she was fully dressed.

"It smells like Daddy," she said as she settled in.

I wanted so badly to believe that, but it had been a month since Joel was in our bed.

"It does," I said, stroking her hair. "Smells just like him."

My sister left the room, and Sophie and I stayed like that for a long time. I gave her tickles. I stroked her hair. I kissed the top of her head as we both snuggled with Joel's pillow and cried.

"I miss him," she said.

"I know you do, sweetness," I said. "Me, too."

I could hear people in the house. I tried to imagine what Joel would think of all of this. We were known for throwing great parties. *It's a good one,* I told him. *You'd be so happy.*

There's an expression I heard once that goes something like, if you act *as if* then you will create the reality. So if you acted *as if* you were successful, you'd become successful. If you acted *as if* you had a social life, you'd have a social life. If you acted *as if* you could survive the loss of *your person,* you would.

When Joel was in the hospital and his death was looming, my *as if* was a phrase I would repeat often to myself. I now said it in a whisper to Sophie.

I held her under the covers, my mouth close to her ear.

"We're going to be OK," I said. "We're going to be OK."

TEN

Only Child, Only Parent

In the dark weeks that followed, there were beacons of light shining a path for Sophie and me to follow. Jillian and Ellie had set up a meal train to alleviate the burden of making dinner every night. Friends of mine from New York sent me restaurant gift cards. Another friend sent us gift certificates for manicures. Others offered to come over and do our laundry or walk the dogs. People were thinking of us, sending us their love, and we felt it.

One day a package came in the mail from a fellow writer friend. In it were two copies of *Healing After Loss: Daily Meditations for Working Through Grief* by Martha Whitmore Hickman. One for me, one for Sophie. Each page contained a meaningful quote, an anecdote, and a short meditation.

Every night before lights out, Sophie and I would read the day's page out loud to each other. I would often cry. Some passages resonated, others not so much. We would follow the reading with a memory each of us had of Joel.

"He hated cilantro," Sophie might say.

"Daddy loved taking you to school every morning," I might say.

And so it went. Every night for almost a year. I was adamant about it, and if for some reason we went to sleep at different times or were too exhausted to stay up an extra five minutes, I made sure we would read the night we missed the following night, too. The ritual of it—reading, reflecting, sharing our memories of Joel—was crucial to my healing.

Otherwise, I kept acting *as if* things were normal, and it's because of Sophie that I was able to pretend they were. She had a schedule; she had school commitments. She needed me to keep her on track, the same as it had always been. I was able to get her to school on time, to make her meals, to help with homework . . . I was able to focus on her, instead of how alone and scared I felt.

I seemed to cry every day, all day long and well into the night, but I feared Sophie wasn't crying enough. *Is she shutting down?* I wanted her to have peers to talk to, but we didn't know other kids who had lost a parent. Her teachers and the school counselor welcomed her back to school and were sensitive to her situation. So were her fellow classmates and friends. They were so sensitive, in fact, that none of them even mentioned what happened. It was confusing. She was afraid of what people might say, but they said nothing. Which in some ways was worse. She was in eighth grade. The brink of adolescence. In middle school the goal is to be just like everyone else. But Sophie was now "the girl whose dad died."

"It's so weird," she told me over dinner one night. "Other than the twins who wanted to talk to me about their goldfish dying, no one ever mentions Daddy."

"They just don't know what to say," I offered.

"But it'd be easier if they said something instead of just ignoring it."

I had heard about a grief camp for kids who had lost a family member. Not necessarily a parent—it could be a sibling or a cousin or even a grandparent. It took place over one weekend in the summer, but applications were due in the spring. Sophie absolutely refused to go.

"I think it would be really good for you to meet other kids in a similar situation," I said.

"Maybe if I had a friend to go with, but I don't want to go alone."

I often thought how things would be different if she did have a sibling. It was in these moments when I wished more than anything that she did. Someone to commiserate with and share in this tragedy with. Someone who was close in age, someone on her level, so she didn't feel like the only thirteen-year-old in the world who this had happened to.

I made an appointment for us with Cheryl, a therapist I had started seeing earlier in the year when the MS was at its worst. If Sophie wasn't going to go to a grief camp or a grief group, then I wanted her to have someone other than me to talk to.

As we sat on Cheryl's couch together, I mentioned my concern that we were grieving so differently. I explained why I felt it was important for Sophie to have someone to share her feelings with. Cheryl listened to me while also keeping an eye on Sophie, who sat quietly, staring at her hands.

During a pause from my soliloquy, Cheryl looked at her and said, "You know, Sophie, I don't usually talk about myself in here, but I want to share something with you."

Sophie looked up at her, her expression unchanged.

Cheryl continued. "I lost my father when I was the same age as you."

Sophie gasped and sat up in her seat a little taller. Even though some of her grandparents had suffered the loss of a parent in their childhoods, hearing it from this stranger, who had a nice office, and was a kind person, was reassuring. I saw a flash on Sophie's face, a reckoning that perhaps this was something that she, too, might survive. Sophie quietly started to cry. I squeezed her hand.

Because Cheryl was my therapist, we agreed it would be better for Sophie to see Julie, a therapist in training who was still working on getting her certification hours. Julie was young and pretty, with long dark hair and big brown eyes, and she had a tattoo. Sophie liked her immediately. Cheryl was Julie's supervisor, so I knew Sophie would be in good hands.

Jillian came over every Monday. "Melissa Mondays" she called them. She'd bring lunch and help me sort out medical bills and my finances. She called the repair man when my washing machine broke and offered to go with me to the social security office to make sure that Sophie and I received death benefits (an oxymoron if there ever was one).

Ellie took me to the post office and to the market so I wouldn't have to go alone. She also, per my request, told the masses about Joel. My fear was that I'd be at the drugstore, or the dry cleaners, or somewhere with Sophie, and run into someone who didn't know. I didn't want to have to explain or say the words *Joel died* if someone were to ask me, *How's your husband doing?*

We had open invitations, no matter the day or hour, to our friends' homes and family events. Our neighbor Roxanne would often ring the bell and simply sit with us and play with the dogs, just so our house had some life to it.

Regardless of the love and support and care we were given, I was overwhelmed with what my life now was. Money was a concern. I had written a script before Joel was admitted to the hospital, but the thought of pursuing that now had me reeling. Even when I had been working steadily and had been nominated for prestigious awards, every meeting was a question of *What have you written or worked on lately?* For me, *lately* had been a long time.

I hadn't worked a "real job" in years. Ellie and I had dissolved our business, and I no longer had any kind of career or even a resume. As a longtime freelancer, I was accustomed to months of not working, but without Joel's steady income I was worried how I would manage financially. So many widows and widowers have financial concerns. There may be mouths at home to feed and bills to pay. It's the trickle-down effect of losing your partner. Financial worries only add to the stress of grief.

As a writer and entrepreneur, I was underqualified *and* overqualified for most jobs. I had no experience in the retail or service industry, and yet I didn't have the right kind of skills for an office job. Trying to get a writing job outside of TV and film was also challenging. I spoke screenwriting fluently, but I wasn't up to speed on writing content for online platforms, where a background in marketing was a qualification I didn't have or even understand. Not only were my options limited, but I wanted to be available for Sophie as much as possible. I wanted to take her to school, and I wanted to be there when she came home, have dinner together, help with homework (if she would let me).

Joel had been the co-owner of a small music marketing company. His friend Ben was the other owner but was a silent partner who left Joel to run the day-to-day operations. Joel had two other full-time employees working underneath him.

I remember calling Ben early one morning while Joel was still at the first hospital.

"I think we're going to transfer him," I said. "His doctors think there's a better chance at recovery if we get him to his MS doctors."

"OK." Ben considered. "Well, I'm pretty sure the crew at the office can handle things this week until Joel gets back."

Tears poured out of my eyes. I shook my head. *How can I convey what I need to?*

"Ben," I said. "I don't think you understand. I don't know when Joel will be back. I don't know *if* he'll be back. Whatever this is, it's serious."

"OK." I could hear Ben's mind spinning through the phone. He took a breath and said, "Let's think positive. If anyone is determined to bounce back after a setback like this, it's Joel."

Ben, like everyone else, couldn't grasp the gravity of the situation. It was too surreal. Ben and Joel had known each other from the music industry long before they went into business together. Joel had been the best man at Ben's wedding.

With Joel now gone, Ben and I had to discuss the future of their business. With Ben's time being spent on his other professional endeavors, could the company continue without Joel? Because the music industry had changed so much since they started the company, their once robust enterprise was now earning half of what it used to. Closing shop would mean Joel's two employees—his close friends—would be out of a job.

After much consideration, we decided to keep the business going. In large part this was to ensure that I could receive a stipend that would allow me to be as present in Sophie's life as I wanted to be. It was the move of a true mensch, and provided me with a financial cushion that gave me room to breathe. Joel's friends were determined to sustain the business, not just for their own benefit but for mine and Sophie's as well. It was Joel's legacy.

Still, I put a tremendous amount of pressure on myself to continue *living* my life without Joel. He liked that I was a strong and independent woman. But his love and support are where I got so much of my strength from.

"Hun," Joel said one night. "I have an idea."

He had just arrived home from work and was planning to walk the dogs. Meanwhile, I was staring into the fridge, stressed out. I had no idea what to make for dinner.

"So do I. Why don't you do the cooking every night?" I was angry. I hated cooking. I made the same three things until we got sick of it. I'd find something new but Sophie wouldn't want to eat it, Joel was always trying to eat healthier, and I couldn't reconcile our different preferences. Cooking took time and effort, and it was always met with some disappointment.

"I can't take it!" I said.

"Here's my idea. I know you're going to hate it, but hear me out."

I started to make a frozen pizza. "Sorry. It's the best I can do," I said as I put it in the oven.

He put his hands on my shoulders. "Breathe," Joel said.

"What's your idea?"

"Let's do something like Taco Tuesdays or Pasta Thursdays? Maybe Salmon Sundays every week. We can plan meals so you don't get so stressed out about dinner all the time."

"Salmon Sundays?" I smirked.

"I think a schedule will take some of the pressure off of you. Believe me, if we could afford to hire a personal chef, I would. Mostly for you."

I was good at being a wife and mother. I loved our little family. I just couldn't stand the cooking part. I sighed and pulled Joel into a hug.

"You're delicious," I told him. "I should make you for dinner every night."

"Trust me," Joel said. "Taco Tuesday will make life easier. For all of us."

If I could barely manage dinner without him, how was I going to do anything?

And more importantly, how was I supposed to raise Sophie on my own? I worried over my ability to give her the skills to be a well-adjusted, happy, and successful person. How was I going to be the one to guide her in choosing the right friends, the right kind of life partner, the right profession? Where was the guarantee that she would be able to function in the world and be fulfilled, productive, and again, happy?

I was left with this precious being, who had lost the most important male figure of her entire life, who made her feel loved and special and important. And he was gone.

Sophie was an only child. I was now an only parent.

I did not have the luxury of co-parenting with my husband. I was a full-time parent, twenty-four hours a day, seven days a week. By myself. It all seemed daunting. After thirteen years with Joel by my side, I did not have the confidence that I would be able to raise our daughter alone and be good at it.

Sophie and I traveled a lot that first year. It was easier to be away from home. One of Sophie's best friend's parents were divorced, and I was friendly with the mom. She and her daughter were heading to Hawaii for winter break, and I invited us to join them. Joel had only been gone for two months, but they didn't seem fazed that they would be spending their vacation with a brand-new widow and half an orphan.

We were perfect travel companions. The moms spent days by the pool while the girls went paddle boarding and swimming. We shared some dinners and sat on the beach while the girls took a surf lesson. We were busy but relaxed in a tropical paradise, and my friend never seemed to mind that throughout most of it, I was present but not really there. She didn't seem to mind that sometimes I would stop mid-conversation and put on my sunglasses to hide my tears. She didn't mind that dinner plans were cancelled last minute because Sophie and I were too sad to leave our room. She didn't seem to mind that on the white sandy beaches of Oahu's North Shore, Sophie and I were arguing.

"This is a great place to sit and just think about Daddy and how much he loved the ocean."

"You don't have to tell me when to think about Daddy," Sophie said.

But I couldn't help myself. "I just would like you to spend some time reflecting on the time we all had together."

"God, Mom. Stop telling me how to feel!"

I didn't mean to.

My brain had a hard time reconciling that Joel was missing. There were people all around us, everywhere we went, but none of them were my husband. *Where is he?*

I would look to Sophie to commiserate, but she didn't have a need to discuss Joel as much as I did. I kept trying to elicit a response from her, maybe even some emotion. She seemed to hold a lot inside, and this concerned me. My tears were plentiful and unpredictable. I rarely saw her cry.

I thought if I just kept us *busy, busy, busy* and distracted—*if we just keep moving*—maybe we would forget for a few hours just how hard it was to move through life without Joel.

ELEVEN

The Other Joel

When Joel was in a coma, newly admitted to the second hospital, I came home one day to make a quick turnaround before picking Sophie up from school. I went inside, put down the ubiquitous medical paperwork from the day, splashed my face with water, and rushed outside to get back in the car for school pickup. In that short amount of time, a package had been delivered and was waiting for me on the front porch. I wasn't expecting anything and didn't even hear the dogs barking that someone had been out front. I picked it up, curious, and saw the Bravo TV logo on it. The package was in a soft wrapping, and as I started to open it, I remembered.

"I know what I want for my birthday!" I had said to Joel over lunch in our kitchen a few weeks earlier.

"You do?" he asked. I rarely wanted anything other than a meal at a nice restaurant.

"A mazel sweatshirt," I said.

"OK, from where?" Then it registered. "Wait, what?"

"From Bravo TV. Bravo-wear, it's called."

Mazel is the Jewish word for luck or congratulations, and the sweatshirt I yearned for had the word *mazel* emblazoned on it.

He shook his head, smiling. "Is that like a *Real Housewives* thing?"

"Kind of?" I said, but it sounded more like a question.

Joel laughed. "OK. Send me a link or something, and we'll see."

I hugged him and said, "You."

He wasn't doing great at the time. Just that morning, the nurse had given him his first round of steroid infusions. He thought he would try to get some work done that afternoon . . . which is when I slipped a note under the office door with the details.

I didn't know he had ordered it, and Joel would never know I received it. He would never know how happy it made me, even when I wore it to the hospital the next day to show him. I sobbed into the sweatshirt that afternoon.

That was the last birthday gift I would ever receive from Joel. I decided it was a sign of Joel's love for me. In his absence, I started looking for signs everywhere.

~

I focused all of my attention on Sophie. She motivated me to keep going, because without Joel, I felt like half a person. I was only half paying attention. Half listening. Doing everything half-assed. Sophie had lost her father, and now only had half a mother.

She was seeing her therapist once a week. Julie's office was a twenty-minute drive away. So instead of taking Sophie to a soccer game or drama class, like Joel and I had done every Saturday for most of her childhood, our Saturday mornings were now spent going to therapy. Sometimes we'd pick up a smoothie or a coffee drink on the way. I would drop her off and park the car where I would stay for the next fifty minutes. I usually spent the time on the phone with my dad and Elisabeth. Sometimes I would visit Hal and Rita, who lived nearby. But more times than not, I would sit in the car and listen to satellite radio. I'd catch up on Howard Stern or the Oprah station.

One Saturday morning, while perusing the channels, I heard a voice that made me stop turning the dial. It sounded happy, like he was smiling while talking. I caught the tail end of the program and could tell that this man's eyes twinkled, much the way Joel's did. Then an announcer interrupted the program.

"Stay tuned, and Joel will be right back with another message of inspiration for an empowered and spirit-filled life!"

Had I been driving, I would have crashed the car. My heart started racing and tears were pouring down my face.

"Hun?!" I cried out. "Is that you? Oh my God, Joel?! I'm here, honey. I'm staying tuned. Oh my God, come back!"

I rolled up the windows in the car, and I turned up the volume. I gripped the steering wheel, tap-tap-tapped my foot anxiously awaiting Joel's return; I was careful to avoid the brake and gas pedals. My body couldn't contain my excitement. I wanted to hear Joel's message! It couldn't have been more clear—Joel was trying to reach me!

A million thoughts swirled in my mind. He was going to tell me something. Maybe that Sophie would be OK, that she was doing great. Or maybe it was about our dog Daisy, who was sick. Or maybe he wanted to tell me that he missed me, too. I wiped away my tears, *waiting, waiting, waiting* for Joel's message.

Finally, *finally!* Joel came back on air. "God bless you. It's a joy to come into your home. Thanks so much for tuning in and coming out today."

Hmmmm, I thought. *God bless you?*

The message continued. "I like to start with something funny." *Yup, that's my Joel!*

And then Joel went on to tell a story about an old man who ran into his doctor at a park. The man was with an attractive young woman. He tells his doctor, "I did what you told me and got myself a hot mama."

The doctor says, "No, what I told you is that you've got a heart murmur!" *OK, not my husband's best joke but . . .*

"Hold up your bible. Say it like you mean it: This is my bible. I am what it says I am. I have what it says I have . . . I boldly confess my heart is receptive . . ."

Bible? I was so confused. This didn't really sound like my Joel. "In Jesus's name, God bless you."

Did Joel find Jesus?! I was intrigued. This couldn't be *my* Joel, but I continued listening. I looked at my dashboard. The radio display had been blank, but now, possibly because of better reception or possibly because I was now receiving the sign I was so desperate for, the screen was lit up. And there he was, right in front of me. *Joel Osteen.*

I had heard of him but never *heard* him. A few months before, my instinct would have been *Ew, evangelical preacher-man. Change the channel.* But I kept listening. I found Joel's message of love soothing. He was saying something about the goodness of God.

That we are *strong, blessed. We are all God's masterpiece.*

That we are all *armed with strength for every battle,* and that *the forces that are for me are greater than those against me.*

I was in agreement with what he was saying. I found that his voice and disposition made me smile. He seemed like someone I would like.

This "new" Joel and my Joel both had dark hair. Joel Osteen had a twinkle in his blue eyes, the way my Joel had a twinkle in his green eyes. He also had the same initials as my Joel, and they even had similar sounding last names. But the thing that I took as the biggest message was this: Both Joels had the same phone number. With the exception of the area code, they were exactly the same.

"Guess what my new number is?" Joel had called to tell me many years earlier. Back when cell phones were new*ish.* "555-JOEL. That makes it so easy to remember!" He was so excited by this. It was fun.

Some people say they found God just walking down the street and boom! They are touched and converted and become born-again or Christ loving or true believers. They get *on board with the Lord,* no questions asked.

That's not what happened to me. I did not find God that day in my car, but I did find something. A connection. Just like when my Joel told me something funny about John Cougar Mellencamp in the mail room so long ago, I was now smitten with a new Joel. I didn't take his bible and Jesus speak as proselytizing (even though it was). I simply liked his energy. His enthusiasm. His message, which was one of trusting in something bigger than ourselves. Believing that we are loved, unconditionally. He preached *an attitude of gratitude*. These were things I could wrap my mind around. To me, Joel Osteen is a motivational speaker who uses God and Jesus as his point of reference. I didn't mind one bit.

When Sophie got in the car after therapy, she immediately changed the station.

"Oh, I wanted you to hear that!" I said. "It's a message from Daddy."

"It's no fair!" she whined. "You always get messages, and I don't."

"You get them, too!" I said. "You just don't recognize them yet."

"So what's the message?" she asked.

"OK. I was listening to the radio, and it said that Joel had a message for me. It was Joel Osteen. He's, like, a preacher, but he and Daddy have the same phone number! And he tells funny stories like Daddy—"

"That's not Dad, Mom," she said.

"Well, I'm going to listen to him all the time now. I feel connected."

Sophie rolled her eyes. "He's a preacher? That's just weird. You're being weird."

I shrugged.

What was I going to say? We were nice Jewish girls; she had just been bat mitzvahed less than a year ago. What did we know about Jesus? Or the bible? Maybe I was being weird. But I didn't care. The Other Joel became my obsession. I listened to him *all the time*. I'd pick up Sophie from school extra early just so I could sit in the car and listen to Joel's message before she got in. I'd drive extra slowly wherever I went, just so I could tune in. I signed up for daily email messages, which would thrill me every morning when I opened my mail.

When I mentioned my new Joel to Ellie, she said, "Oh my God, WWJD. What would Joel do?"

When I mentioned it to Jillian, she said, "OK, that's weird. Not that you're listening to him, well that's a little weird, but the phone number, too? Actually, never mind, yes, the whole thing is weird."

When I mentioned it to my sister, she said, "I love him, too! I meant to tell you, I started watching him every Sunday morning. I love Joel!"

We laughed about this. It validated how strange and random this new discovery was.

Not much else held my interest. There's a phenomenon known as "widow brain" or "widow fog." Anyone who's suffered a traumatic loss is likely familiar with this. It's caused by grief. It leaves you feeling dull, confused, and forgetful.

I'd get home from taking the dogs on a walk. I'd still be holding their leashes but had already unlatched the dogs. Or was I holding their leashes because I wanted to *leave* for a walk with them? I couldn't remember if I was coming or going.

Or I would send Sophie a text asking her what she wanted for dinner. But by the time I got to the market, I would forget. I'd stare at her response on my phone for five minutes in the produce section, chicken. But I didn't know what chicken meant.

I was always distracted. I moved slower than usual. I wasn't processing.

I could no longer read, even though I was an avid reader and always had a stack of books on my nightstand. My book club, which I had started and led, fell apart. A passage from our grief healing book was just about all I could manage. That and the inspirational bite-size nuggets I received via email from the Other Joel every morning. Even the TV shows that I used to watch with Joel became difficult to bear. They reminded me of him and made me too sad to watch in his absence. Plus, he wasn't there to explain the obvious: *Wait, Don Draper wants to leave Sterling Cooper?* or *OK, remind me why Jon Snow was sent to the wall.*

I blame my widow fog for my increased enthusiasm over *The Real Housewives*, too. I was already a fan of the New York and New Jersey casts, but suddenly the ladies from Beverly Hills piqued my interest. And then Atlanta. It was such mindless entertainment, like, *truly* mindless, that I could actually take it in. If I missed a feud or a confrontation or some dialogue between the women, it really made no difference. All of this "unscripted" drama was a salve to my real-life drama, which wasn't actually that dramatic. It was just that my husband had died. That's all.

I took comfort where I could find it. I found it with Joel Osteen. And also, Iyanla Vanzant. Oh, how I loved Iyanla! This was before she had her own TV show, fixing the lives of fractured families. The Iyanla whom I loved spoke "universe" and spirit. I first saw her on the *Oprah Winfrey Show*, of course way back in the early days, and I loved her then. But I rediscovered her when Joel died. I was in my neighborhood bookstore, *searching, searching, searching* for something that could help me with my grief. I had my journals, which I wrote in consistently, but I needed to hear someone else's voice, someone else's perspective, someone who had walked a similar path.

There were a few books on "young" widowhood with cheeky titles, but they did nothing for me. I couldn't relate. I was selfish in my grief, maybe even a little self-centered. No one experienced *my* grief because they weren't married to Joel. They didn't know what it felt like to have the man you love make you coffee every morning when he wasn't even a coffee drinker. They didn't know what it felt like to be married to a person who not only made you laugh out loud every day but also left Post-it notes with sketches around the house that declared his love for you, calling you beautiful, with drawings and doodles of connected hearts, just because. They didn't know what it felt like *to feel love* on that level, every single day.

Something on the bookstore shelf caught my eye. *Peace from Broken Pieces: How to Get Through What You're Going Through* by Iyanla Vanzant. Strangely, I found it in the cooking section.

I was still tortured by cooking every meal, and I wanted to find a user-friendly cookbook. It was challenging cooking for two. It was there that Iyanla's book found me. It must have been accidentally placed there, and I took it as a sign.

I sat down in the middle of the aisle to read the prologue. I learned that Iyanla's daughter had died. I tucked that book under my arm and found another of hers, *Yesterday, I Cried*, in its rightful place in the self-help section. I bought them both.

Iyanla wrote about lessons learned from hardships, about the abundance of opportunities to heal our broken hearts, and that wisdom can be found in our buckets full of tears.

Her writing was different. It was personal. I felt connected to it. I could read a paragraph a day, and the words were so resonant that that was enough for me. I added Iyanla to my healing arsenal that now included Joel Osteen and *The Real Housewives*.

I didn't know that I was "healing," but I knew that I was broken. Knowing that God, love, the universe, or spirit *had* me, helped me move slightly easier through the world.

"Mom?" Sophie asked me one night after she shared her memory. (*Daddy wanted me to watch* The Graduate *with him. It was his favorite movie.*) "Where do you think Daddy is?"

I was lying next to her, stroking her hair. "I wish I knew. But I think he's feeling better, wherever he is."

"Why do you think that?" She wanted to know.

"I just do. I think our bodies are temporary. And his body was so sick. Now that he's not in his body, he must feel better, right? I just have to believe that."

"I think he's here with us," she said.

"You do?"

She nodded yes.

"That makes me so happy," I said. "Even when you and I are apart, Daddy will still be with you, and with me. He'll always be watching over you and protecting you, like an angel."

I told her this every night for months. I don't know that Sophie took it in the way I meant it. I sometimes think she just said what she thought I wanted to hear just so she could go to sleep.

I visited a psychic the spring after Joel had died. The appointment was made months earlier. Maybe it's a phenomenon only in Los Angeles, but similar to getting a reservation at a great restaurant, the best psychics in LA book up months in advance.

I was not new to the world of psychics. In fact, one of the best readings I had was when I was in my early twenties and living in New York City. I had only just had the *thought* that I may want to try my hand at screenwriting, when the psychic my friend told me that I *must see* had an opening. I was looking for some direction—*Should I stay in New York and work in advertising, or should I consider going back to Los Angeles and attempt screenwriting? Would I find love again in the city or back in my hometown?* I believed that Katherine might have the answers.

The doorman in Katherine's opulent eastside building showed me to the elevator, which took me up to the penthouse. Her assistant led me to one of the bedrooms, where a card table was set up next to a king-size bed that was covered in satin pillows of all shapes and sizes. At the card table sat Katherine—blonde, big, friendly. Think *Texas*. But this was New York City, and Katherine was all business.

I was there for five minutes when Katherine, without knowing anything about me, said, "I see you in these big warehouses. There are big cameras and lights, too."

"Really?" I said.

"And something about foxes. Or a fox. Fox and . . ." She was searching, concentrating; her eyes closed. "Fox, fox. They keep showing me a fox. But also, lights, big lights, movie lights."

I was trying to figure out what she meant. *Foxes?* My mind came up blank. The closest thing I could think of were the deer we'd sometimes see on weekends in the Hamptons. But I stayed quiet. Then Katherine's eyes opened, and she smiled and looked at me.

"Fox," she said. "And Disney. You'll be working for them. Writing. I see pages, lots of pages everywhere, *so much writing*! That's what they're telling me. You are a writer!"

I didn't quite understand who "they" were. But I took what she was saying as the confirmation I needed at the time. *I am a writer!*

Or at least, I would *be* a writer at some point in the future.

Sure enough, when I moved back to Los Angeles later that year, my first employer was Disney. Followed by Fox. Later, Disney again. I don't remember much else from that reading with Katherine, but clearly it didn't dissuade me from believing that some people have a gift, a gift that allows them to tune into a frequency that relays messages from somewhere beyond. This is what I was hoping for when I drove to Beverly Hills to meet Candy, the psychic I waited almost five months to see.

"Come in," Candy said. "We've been waiting."

Candy's office was in a big building in Beverly Hills. The other occupants seemed to be doctors. Candy sat at a desk full of family photos and trinkets. She had more framed photos on the walls; some were of her posing with celebrities.

She gestured for me to sit across from her, and she smiled warmly. She had a full figure and an enthusiastic energy.

"Yes, oh my God, he's been waiting for you!" She started to laugh and looked up like she was talking to the air. "She's here, she's here. Oh my God, he's so happy!" She looked at me and asked, "What did you bring me?" She had a vague accent, somewhere from the Middle East, I thought. Israel or maybe Iran.

I reached into my bag. Psychics sometimes suggest bringing an object or a photo of the person you hope to connect with. It helps them channel or receive information. I handed her Joel's watch—a gift from his father years earlier that Joel had worn every day. I also brought some photos. She looked at one of them.

"This is him?" she asked.

So far, all I had said was hello.

"He was sick. So sick. I thought he was older . . . Now I'm confused."

"Yes," I said. "That's my husband."

"So young!" she said. She got very serious staring at his picture. "He went very quickly. He was waiting to go."

I started to cry.

"It's funny because my client before you, she's been waiting for a man to come into her life, and your husband was here waiting for you. She was so disappointed, but I knew he wasn't here for her. She was hoping because this man, your husband . . . His love is . . ." She searched for the word.

"Strong. His love is very strong for you. I thought he was older because of the sickness."

She continued to concentrate. She stroked the photo with her index finger.

"He couldn't move?" she asked. "Not the coma, I mean, in life."

I hadn't said anything about a coma.

"He had MS. So, yes, moving was difficult," I answered through my tears.

"Ooh," she said as if she had finally gotten an answer she was looking for. "He can move now, my dear. He's so happy; he has his legs. And his bike. Did he like to ride a bike?"

Before I could answer, Candy smiled and giggled a little.

"Oh my God, he's stroking your face right now. He loves you so much."

I put my hand on my cheek. I closed my eyes. I could picture Joel standing there, his hand on my cheek, my hand on his hand.

"Who is the boy?" she asked.

"What boy?"

"Do you have a son?" she asked me inquisitively.

"No," I said, suddenly nervous. I wanted to hear more about Joel. All of this information was coming at me so fast. I wanted her to slow down.

"There's another man. With a son. I can't believe this!"

Candy started laughing again. "You are blessed, you know this? This man with a son. He loves you, too."

I looked at her as if another head were growing from her neck.

"What man?" I said.

"Someone you know," she continued. "But it won't last long. That's what your husband is telling me. But he doesn't mind. It's OK."

What the hell? Another man? Who has a son?! I don't want another man. I just want Joel!

"I don't think I want another man," I said.

She shrugged. "What can I tell you? He's coming."

Candy tilted her head as if she were listening. "Maybe this will make sense. Your husband wants me to tell you . . ."

I sat up taller in my seat, leaned in a little closer.

"'I approve,' he's saying. He approves."

She opened her palms and raised her eyebrows as if to say, *There you have it.*

Two things were made clear to me that day.

1. Joel really was still with us. I could go home to Sophie and tell her. I was so excited! *Daddy's really with us!* I would say, *He's here!*

And

2. Psychics are nuts.

TWELVE

I'm a Widow

S issy?" I said into the phone, unable to catch my breath. "I miss Joel!"

"Oh, sissy," Holly said patiently. "I know you do."

It was our wedding anniversary, my first without him. We would have been married seventeen years. I was sobbing uncontrollably in my hotel room and had been for hours. I was in Chicago visiting my friend Jennie. Sophie was on a school field trip to San Francisco that weekend, so the timing worked out for me to get out of town. I did not want to be home without Joel on our anniversary. I thought being away with one of my best friends, in one of my favorite cities, at a fancy hotel I decided to treat myself to, would help. But grief doesn't care about any of those things. Just like MS, it travels with you no matter where you go, no matter how far, no matter for how long.

Jennie and her husband had planned to take me to dinner. They were downstairs in the hotel bar waiting for me.

"I'm not sure if I can make it," I had cried into the phone an hour earlier to Jennie. "I'm a mess. I can't stop crying."

"OK, I totally get it. We'll wait in the bar, and if you feel like you can pull it together, great. If not, no pressure. Just keep me posted."

I thought I would spend my anniversary walking down Michigan Avenue, stopping at a cute café for lunch, buying something nice for myself, and reflecting on my seventeen years with Joel—more if I counted our time together before we got married. Instead, I had left the hotel without an umbrella, got stuck in the rain, got lost trying to find a nice day spa where I could get a massage, and ended up back at the hotel early, soaking wet and sobbing.

"Of course you're feeling sad," Holly said. "Joel's not there to celebrate with. It's terrible. It's hard to believe."

"I miss him!" I wailed. "I don't know if I'll ever stop crying!"

My sister stayed on the phone with me. I was afraid to hang up. I thought my tears would envelop me, that I might drown.

I kept twisting my wedding ring around my finger, hoping that my memories of Joel—younger, healthy, *alive*—would come back to me. I tried so hard to remember my wedding. Our life together. The way he smelled. But five months later, I could still only remember Joel in the hospital. Barely alive, waiting for me to give the OK so he could die. The only smells I could conjure were the hospital smells. The only memory of us being close was holding Joel's limp hand in mine, trying to avoid the tubes in his veins. I could not get out of the hospital, as hard as I tried. I could talk about Joel and recall certain events spent with him, but they were dulled. I kept waiting for my memories to become vibrant and real again.

Holly and I eventually hung up. Jennie sent her husband home, and she came up to my room. She, too, was patient. She had lost her mother when she was young, so she understood what grief was like and that it was unpredictable.

After crying for hours and hours, I forced myself to change my thinking. *I can cry anywhere at any time. You're in Chicago, go do something fun,* I told myself. *That's what you'd do if Joel were here.*

So Jennie and I went down to the hotel restaurant and got some food. I got a fancy cocktail, and we toasted Joel. My tears had subsided.

I was breathing again. I slept well that night, but I woke up with a grief hangover. I wasn't quite myself. My widow fog was clouding my weekend, but it was time to get back home.

On my way to the airport, I made a stop at a sandwich place that Joel had loved to go to when we were in Chicago. I went for Joel. But now I was late for my flight. I had never seen O'Hare so packed. One of the luggage screeners was broken, so the security line was taking an extralong time. I watched Jennie drive away, and started wheeling my bag to the end of the line when the tears started again. I stood in that security line and realized I would be there for two hours and my flight was leaving in one.

I noticed a gruff TSA officer pacing the line. His belly hung over his belt. His hair was thinning, but his bushy mustache made up for it. He was making sure that we, the travelers, were staying in line and following the rules. A few people were understandably annoyed. They tried to get his attention. Some of them, like me, were afraid of missing their flights. Others were simply aggravated by the bureaucracy of airport security. It was tense. I noticed all of this going on around me, but I just stood there crying. Bereft. Tired. Empty.

The TSA guy must have noticed me. He approached me with . . . the only word I can come up with is *caution*. I think he was afraid of a woman in tears. Not just tears, a flood on her face.

"Why ya cryin' so hard?" he asked me.

I looked at him blankly. I saw him. I knew he was talking to me. But I couldn't respond.

This had happened to me once before. Joel and I were on a ski trip with friends in Lake Tahoe. After a day spent mostly on my ass, attempting to learn how to snowboard in a blizzard, I had had enough. I had fallen one time too many and was done. I couldn't move from weariness. Ski patrol had to come and get me and bring me down the hill on one of their little red sleds. Joel, of course, accompanied me down. He was worried. In all my years on skis, nothing like this had ever happened.

We got to the first aid hut. The nurse started asking me questions: "Can you tell me what day it is?"

I heard her question, but I was too tired to answer. I stared at her blankly.

"Do you know where you are?"

I simply couldn't talk. I felt Joel squeeze my hand.

"What is your name?"

I half smiled. It was the best I could do.

The nurse turned to Joel and asked, "Does she speak English?"

I began to laugh. What started out as a giggle turned into full-on hysterics. My entire body shook. I looked crazy. I couldn't catch my breath from laughing so hard. I found that last question to be so outrageous. *Do I speak English? Really? Am I that far gone?* I laughed myself better. Joel couldn't help but laugh, too.

"Yes, she speaks English," he managed to say.

"Yes, yes, yes!" I said. "I can answer all of your questions. I just needed a minute." I cackled.

"Thank goodness!" that nice nurse said. "You had me worried." She started laughing, too.

Without Joel next to me, though, I didn't think I could ever be me again.

I didn't know how to respond to the TSA guy who stood there looking at me, cautiously.

"Ya alright, there?" he asked me again.

People were staring at me. I noticed the clock; my flight was now leaving in forty-five minutes, and I was nowhere near the front of the line. I tried to think of something to say. I needed help. I couldn't miss my flight home. I took a deep breath, wiped my face with the back of my hand, and without thinking, said something I had never said before:

"I'm a widow."

The TSA guy and I shared the same expression, which was: surprise. It was the first time I had said it out loud. The TSA guy, whose name tag said *John*, gave me the once over and I understood why. Out of all the things I could have been crying about, being a widow probably didn't cross his mind.

"Jesus," he said. "I'm sorry."

"I need to get home to my daughter," I cried.

"Of course you do. Come on."

It's possible, given my emotional state, that he thought I had just been widowed that day. I didn't bother to clarify. John opened up a space in the rope and let me through. He reached for my suitcase, and I let him take it.

"Which flight you trying to catch?" he asked.

"To Los Angeles," I told him.

He whistled. "Cutting it close."

John led me through to the front of the line, easily passing a hundred other people.

"Ya gonna be OK," John said as he lifted my bag onto the security belt for screening. I couldn't tell if he was asking me or telling me.

"Thank you so much," I told him as I walked through the scanner. "Really," I said through my tears. "That was really nice."

He nodded from the other side of security. He called after me, "Get home safe. God bless."

I took that blessing. I felt it and luckily made my flight.

Back in LA, I called Jillian on the way home from the airport. She asked about my trip.

"It was great but terrible," I told her. "I loved seeing Jennie but I cried the whole time. I missed Joel . . . But I figured something out."

"What?" she asked.

"Are you sitting down?"

"Yes!" she said.

"Jill." I paused. "Guess what?"

"What?" she asked.

Then I said it. "I'm a widow!"

I could practically see her take the phone away from her ear and stare at it. She either thought I was crazy or stupid. She knows I'm not stupid.

"Um, yes. I think I knew that," she said.

"No, you knew, but you didn't *know*. I'm a widow!"

"Huh," she said. "Give me a minute to think about that."

I waited. Looked out the window. Yawned.

"OK," she said a minute later. "I do get that now. Wow. You're right. I can't believe it either!"

"Right?!"

It was a revelation. The word suddenly felt different. I may not have looked like a widow, but I felt like one. *Widow* once described a much older woman. Old, wrinkled, tragic. Wearing black. Maybe even a veil. I felt like a version of Charles Dickens's jilted old Miss Havisham, but instead of being left at the altar and staying in my wedding dress forever, I was left in midlife, barefoot in shiva clothes and a blowout.

Once I started referring to myself as a widow, I couldn't stop. I don't know what took me so long to claim it. That's what it felt like; that I was *claiming* the word, asserting some truth about myself because it wasn't obvious if you looked at me. And in saying it, declaring it, embracing it, I was convincing myself that it was real. Joel was gone. He was still my husband. We were still married, but I was a widow.

A widow.

I'd be at the car wash, and while waiting for our cars, the person next to me might say something like, *Last time I got a car wash, it rained the next day.*

I'd reply, *Oh, I hate it when that happens. Especially because I'm a widow.*

Or, Sophie and I would be at the In-N-Out Burger drive-through. I'd give our order through the speaker. *We'll take one double-double, two large fries, and two chocolate shakes . . . because I'm a widow.*

Sophie would roll her eyes, mortified. "M-o-o-o-m!"

"Maybe they'll throw in something free!" I'd say to her as we drove to the pay window. "Some sympathy fries or something." They never did.

Once when I took the dogs to the groomers, and they said they'd be ready at three o'clock, I replied, "No problem. I'm a widow; I'll be here at three!"

The word didn't scare me. It didn't make me cower. It gave me something to say, a way to place myself in the world. I had a word for what I was, and I used it. It felt powerful.

When I dropped the word, and the stranger realized that I said *widow*, I would see the wheels in their mind spinning, waiting to register. Once it did, they would stare at me, stunned, confused. *I never would have guessed!* someone once said. Maybe that's why I felt compelled to tell people, to say it out loud. Saying I was a widow made it real. For me, it was impossible to understand that my husband died. It made no sense. We were supposed to grow old together. We shared a life. We loved *and* liked each other. It's not that I wanted people to know, I *needed* them to.

Everyone in my neighborhood, of course, already knew. Some decided I was in need of not just their condolences but their sympathy. I was once at Trader Joe's trying to figure out what to make with the chicken I had just put in my cart when a woman I knew from the neighborhood came up to me crying, tears pouring down her face.

"Melissa." She sniffed. "How *are* you?" She tried to pull me into a hug, but thankfully my shopping cart was in between us. She settled by putting her hands on my arms.

"I'm so sorry. I keep thinking of you and Sophie, and I just keep crying."

This woman was never my favorite. Years ago she had a birthday party for her kindergartner and invited everyone in the entire class. Everyone but Sophie. I'm sure it was an oversight, but I never got over it. So when she came to me crying, I offered no words of comfort (because, *hello, I'm the one who is grieving*) and I didn't feel the need to fill up the space. I preferred it being awkward. I watched her face get red, the tears pouring down. She continued to cry, and then the truth of her being upset really came out.

"I just . . . ," she said with a sob. "I don't know what I would do if it were me."

There. She said it. Her tears, her crying, her sympathy had nothing to do with me. It had to do with *her.* Her fears. Her own anxiety over the possibility, however slim, of losing *her* husband. Having *her* world rocked upside down. I looked at her with indifference.

"Feel better," I said as I wheeled my cart away.

I could own the fact that I was now the town widow, but what I couldn't take was everyone's projections and assumptions. People knew about me, so they thought they *knew* me, thought they knew my story.

They didn't.

They didn't know my suffering or Joel's. They didn't know that I felt like I was grieving long before Joel had even died. That I was grieving before I even *knew* I was grieving.

It's common for widows to feel like they are the ones who need to comfort those who are trying to comfort *them.* I wish I could offer suggestions of the appropriate things to say, but the truth is, I don't know. Grief is personal and private.

For me, I just wanted the acknowledgement (*I'm so sorry* would usually suffice), and depending on the person, I didn't necessarily want much else. I didn't want to make small talk or hear about their eighty-five-year-old aunt who just died in their weak attempt to make their situation relatable to mine.

Nor did I want a hug.

Some people got it just right. Like the time I was doing Clooney, and I saw a woman from the neighborhood who hikes there daily. We aren't friends, but we've known each other for years. She saw me crying, sniffling, working my way up the hill. She was coming toward me in the opposite direction. I didn't want to stop, but I saw her sigh when she saw me. She simply reached out and squeezed my arm as we passed each other. There was no pretense. No over-the-top outburst. My situation was sad. Unbelievable. Hard to fathom . . . and her simple, silent acknowledgement was enough.

Or the friend I ran into from my early days of working at Atlantic with Joel. I barely recognized her; it had been so many years. But she stopped me and said, "I heard about Joel. I'm so sorry." And then continued reminiscing about the old days. I appreciated that she saw my circumstance as a matter of fact. She didn't exude any pity or projections of her own.

People knew Joel and me as a happy couple. They knew us as Sophie's parents. They knew that we lived in the house close to the elementary school (which at one point or another, *everyone* with kids in our neighborhood had parked in front of). But now I was the woman whose husband had died. The husband who everyone saw riding through the neighborhood on his bike. The husband who was so nice. *What did he have again? What was wrong with him? How did he die?*

And if that could happen to me, couldn't it happen to anyone? *How will she manage? In that big house, just her and her daughter? Oh my God! What's she going to do now?*

No one knew what to make of *The Widow*.

The truth is, I didn't know either.

THIRTEEN

Small Steps Forward

H i, this is Allison Frank. I got your name from Rabbi Hannah. My husband died three years ago, and if you ever want to talk to someone, I'd be happy to meet you. Thanks."

I saw the name *Allison Frank* listed as a missed call on my phone, but it would be weeks before I would listen to her message. I let it sit in my inbox because I just wasn't interested. Some friends had told me about Allison. I knew that she lived in our neighborhood, that she had also lost her husband, and that her kids were a little older than Sophie.

I was aware that she might be calling and was encouraged to meet her, but I bristled at the idea. Why in the world would I want to meet anyone else whose husband died? No, I was territorial over my grief. No one but me was married to Joel. No one knew what it felt like to lose their everything.

So I made up my mind to ignore her message. For now.

Besides, it was a busy time. Or at least, a time of transition. Joel had been gone for nearly six months. Everyone knew that Sophie was my priority. In a bit of a role reversal, whenever I was invited anywhere, I would first check with her. I didn't want to leave her alone or with a babysitter. She was getting a bit old for that anyway.

I tended to make my plans during the day, when she was at school. The problem was that friends were inviting me out to dinners. To happy hour. To the theater. I tried; I really tried to just say yes to everything. But the truth is I missed out on many events. The thought of showing up to a friend's fiftieth birthday party by myself, for example, seemed daunting.

I was developing an unhealthy dynamic. I would wait to hear what Sophie's plans were, if any, before making plans for myself. If she was invited to a sleepover on a Friday night, only then would I agree to meet my friends for dinner. If she was going to a movie on a Saturday with one of the grandparents, then I would agree to a hike or to meet someone for coffee.

Everyone was encouraging me to make time for myself. *Happy mom, happy kid,* they'd say. I would try, but how could I ever be happy again given that I was now facing a future without Joel? I was afraid. I didn't know if I would ever feel whole again.

But the truth is, with the exception of my husband dying, my world being completely rocked, and having to do the heavy lifting of two parents, I was a happy person by nature. I had to believe that I could be that way again. It's not that I was no longer laughing or enjoying myself at times, I was, but Joel's absence was always a presence. The minute I would sense it, I'd get sad. It was hard to reconcile.

Leigh, a woman I had known since our daughters were in preschool together, had encouraged me to join her writing group. Leigh's daughter and Sophie had become close friends in middle school, and she and I became close during the girls' bat mitzvah planning and even more so in those difficult months leading up to when Joel was in the hospital, and beyond. Leigh offered an open-door policy to her home at all times. Sophie and I loved the chaos of her house with her three spirited children, doctor husband, and big dog. We could sit there for hours and just watch all of the action. It was so different from our quiet life on our cul-de-sac.

Leigh had a degree in spiritual psychology and shared the same alma matter as one of my "healers," Iyanla Vanzant. You could say she had me at *Iyanla*.

"Look. You're a writer; you should be writing," Leigh told me. "I think it will be very healing for you, and we're a very friendly group. No one bites."

I recognized that I needed to find my way back to myself. Joining a writing group would be a baby step; although, it was also a big one. It meant that I'd actually be getting dressed and leaving the house. But Leigh's presence in the group gave me reassurance. Plus, the class was held in a house in the hills just above my house. I could walk there if I wanted to.

"Soph," I said on the way home from school one day. "I think I'm going to join a writing group."

"OK," she said as she fidgeted with the radio, looking for a good station.

"It meets once a week. Right around the corner from home."

"Uh-huh."

"I'll only be gone for a few hours. I'll leave after dinner and be home by nine thirty, maybe ten, the latest."

I kept driving while Sophie kept changing stations.

"I just think it will be good for me. I haven't written anything in a while, and Leigh's in the class, and I think I just need to start doing stuff again and—"

Sophie took her attention off the radio and glanced at me. "Mom, it's fine."

"You're sure? Because if you'd rather I stay home with you—"

She raised her hands in the air, exasperated. "Oh my God! It's no big deal. Do it. Take a writing class. I'm fine with it!"

I don't know if I was looking for an excuse to get out of it or just making sure she was really OK with my being gone. I asked myself, *WWJD. Hun,* Joel would have said, *do it. You have no excuse not to.*

So I signed myself up to join Leigh's writing group. Every Thursday evening for eight weeks, I drove up the hill. I'd park my car, take a deep breath, and climb up the stairs that led into the house.

The class was composed of about eight people; all were nonprofessional writers. I was the only one who had ever earned a living from my writing, and unfortunately, my worst qualities came out. I was a snob. *What could I possibly learn from people who only write as a hobby?* I had no patience. *You mean every single person is going to read what they wrote? Out loud to the group? And I have to actually pay attention?* And I hated reading what I had only just written. *It hasn't been edited yet; it won't be any good!*

But halfway into the first class, my reservations slipped away. When we went around introducing ourselves that first night, I told them that I was a widow. They reacted in a way that was becoming familiar. I could see them trying to process this information, their smiles fading. *Did she say she's a widow?* And then the questions came. *How old was your husband, if you don't mind us asking? What was the cause of death?* Then the gasps, and condolences, hands on hearts, a few tears were wiped away (including mine), and then we moved on.

Each session started with a five-minute meditation. I didn't mind that. I would try to conjure peaceful thoughts and quiet my mind. I would breathe. Over the course of the first few weeks, I let go of my preconceived ideas about the group. They had interesting things to say. Most could actually *write.* Anna, the group's founder and facilitator, created such a warm and nurturing space, it felt womb-like. I felt a part of something. Something that had nothing to do with being a widow, or a mom, or even a "professional." This was something that was just for me. Just for fun.

Writing was a way back to myself, and the writing group became integral to my well-being. I loved it. The group was supportive and encouraging, the antithesis of what it was like working as a screenwriter where you always felt disposable, underappreciated, and anxious, regardless of how successful you were.

In Anna's group people were writing poetry. Personal essays. Short stories. Romance novels. And I was able to tap into a creative well inside my mind that I forgot existed. I wrote stories and made up scenes. I created characters and built an entire world inhabited by people whom I gave lives to, with children and homes and cars and hobbies. It was exhilarating. Anna's class was the one activity I had planned for myself every week, and I never missed it. When the first eight-week session ended, I signed up again for the next, and the next few sessions after that.

Life was still surreal, but Sophie and I were moving forward. In the tiniest of steps, we were making a life without Joel. I encouraged Sophie to look for him every day, to find him when she needed him, to talk to him. I wanted her to know he was with her, always, and would always love her.

"Daddy loved the Clash," she'd say after reading our nightly passage.

"And the Who," I'd add.

"He looked like Pete Townshend," she'd say.

"And some people thought he looked like Ralph Fiennes," I'd say.

"Who's that?" she'd ask. So I'd pull out my laptop, and we'd go down the rabbit hole of Google images, *searching, searching, searching* for Joel.

I talked to him every day, mostly asking him the same questions: *Where are you? Are you still here? Are you OK?*

Around this time, I also started to get rid of some of Joel's things. It was painful seeing his clothes hanging in the closet next to mine. His toothbrush in its holder on our bathroom counter. His sandals in the basket by the front door. These were constant reminders of his permanent absence. So slowly, I started to assess his things.

Losing Joel cemented the idea that *things* we give such value to are really, truly meaningless. Joel lived. Joel died. And when he died, he took nothing with him. Nothing.

Not his iPad. Not his beloved record collection. Not even his wedding ring.

He took nothing. Because of this, I wasn't particularly attached to the "stuff" left behind. So when I was going through his things, I made piles. Things I knew I wanted to keep for myself and/or for Sophie, and things I wanted to give to family. I liked that people close to us would have something of his. Just like telling everyone that I was a widow, giving away his things kept Joel alive.

My nephew got a casual sports coat and some sweaters. I gave Joel's sister, Andrea, some more of his clothes for her husband and son. Both Hal and Nancy got some photos and other personal things, but it was hardest for them, to see what was left behind. Joel's friends were thrilled to come over and shop his record and CD collection. I loved having his friends over to reminisce with. One thing that surprised me was the amount of guitars and music equipment I found in the garage. Joel liked to strum on the guitar we had in the house, but I had forgotten about all of the other stuff that he had from his band-playing days. There were acoustic guitars, a few electric ones, amplifiers, pedals, chords, even some tambourines.

When I asked Joel's friend Greg what to do with all of it, he suggested that I take it to Guitar Center and that they'd help me out. Another one of Joel's friends agreed. I was in a spring-cleaning mindset and just wanted to be done with this stuff, but with the thought of getting it all in my car, schlepping it across town, not really speaking the "language" of what I had, I decided to just keep it in the garage. I felt overwhelmed by it.

But one night, Jillian asked if I wanted to join her at a concert that one of her friend's sons was playing in. She wanted me to leave my house. To do things for myself. She also knew that I loved music, and this was a low-key event that Sophie's former guitar teacher was putting on with some of his students. I really didn't want to go. I had already been to my writing group that week, and one night out was typically my limit.

Sophie had a starring role in the school musical and was at rehearsals late into the night all week. I had no excuse (other than my husband had died) to say no.

Sophie had taken guitar lessons in seventh grade and stopped a few months before her bat mitzvah. Guitar fell under Joel's jurisdiction. He did all the vetting, set up the schedule, and took her to all of her lessons, which were taught on the other side of our neighborhood.

One day he couldn't make it, so I took her. I parked the car down the street and saw a guy standing in front of a little bungalow, in a T-shirt and jeans with a black beanie on his head and his dark hair sticking out from under it. His face had a strong five o'clock shadow. He was on the phone and waved to Sophie.

"Who is that?" I asked.

"Marcos," she said.

"*That's* the guitar teacher?"

"Yeah."

Marcos was around my age. He was handsome and had a cool, casual musician vibe.

"Have we met before?" he asked as he stuffed his phone into his front pocket. He shook my hand. "You look familiar."

"It's because Sophie and I look so much alike," I answered. I think I may have been blushing.

"You do, but she's got those green eyes like her dad!" he said animatedly. "But yeah, anyway. Thought maybe I knew you."

He opened the front door. "Come on in, Soph. Get yourself set up." Then he turned to me. "Mom, you can have a seat right there." He pointed to his kitchen table, which was just on the other side of the room.

He turned away from me and focused all of his attention on Sophie. "OK, Soph. You been practicing?"

Sophie nodded as she took her guitar out of her case. In amazement, I watched as my twelve-year-old set up her guitar, plugged herself in, and stood in front of the microphone. Marcos took a seat behind the drums, and for the next half hour I watched my daughter have her guitar lesson. They played a few songs, as if they were in a band and had been playing together a long time.

Marcos was a gifted teacher. He treated his students as if they were equals, as if they already knew how to play. It was empowering. I understood why all the kids in the neighborhood who took guitar lessons took them from Marcos.

That night I called our friend who had recommended him, another mom. "No one told me the guitar teacher is so hot!" I said.

She laughed. "Get in line. We all have crushes on Marcos."

The gig Jillian invited me to was in a little club where Joel and I had seen Marcos play, back when he was teaching Sophie. There was a stage and tables; it was set up like a nightclub. It was open to all ages because Marcos wanted kids and their parents to come together to see a rock show, even if the show consisted of Marcos playing with his students. Marcos was a single parent, and his young teenage son would often play these gigs with him.

I remember feeling sad that night, and lonely. I knew almost all of the parents there. They, of course, knew me and Joel. They knew that I was grieving. They were also happy to see me out and about, acting *as if* I had a life. One of the moms gave me a hug. She mentioned her friend Allison, the woman who had left a voicemail for me weeks ago.

"Call her back," said this mom, encouragingly. "Even if you just go for coffee or something, she's great! And she's been through what you're experiencing."

No, she hasn't, I thought. I still held exclusive rights to grief.

"You OK?" Jillian asked.

I nodded my head and looked at the stage as Marcos introduced the eighth grade band. I still found Marcos attractive but was surprised I was capable of noticing.

Jillian and I watched and clapped, and I acted *as if* I was enjoying myself, but after a little while, I turned to her.

"I think I need to go home."

"OK, let's go then," she said a little too fast. This wasn't her scene either, and she understood how hard it was for me.

As we stood up, we noticed Marcos, who was now standing below the stage looking in my direction. "I think he wants to talk to you . . . but he probably doesn't know what to say," Jillian said.

So I approached him. I didn't want to leave without saying hi first.

"Hey there," he said. "How're you doing?"

Before I could answer, Marcos said, "I just want you to know I'm really sorry about Joel. He was a good man. A good father. I saw him in action and . . ." Marcos tapped his heart, emotional.

"Thank you. Yes, we're doing OK," I said.

"Please give Sophie my best, and listen, if there's anything you guys need, anything I can help you with, please don't hesitate, OK? I mean it, anything."

I heard that from a lot of people in those days, offers to help with anything I needed. *But what I need is so much!*

A sense of security.

A sense of well-being.

A sense that I would survive.

In lieu of those elusive things, people genuinely did want to help and were so excited when I gave them something specific: *Can you grab some coffee beans for me next time you're at Costco?* Or, *Would you mind dropping a package off at UPS for me?*

"Actually," I said to Marcos, "I found a bunch of Joel's guitars in our garage. There's a lot of stuff, really. I just . . . I'm not sure what to do with it. Like, if I should try to sell it or maybe your students could use some of it."

"Yeah, I could help with that. But whatever you do, do not take it to Guitar Center."

Few things made me laugh in those days. But his response made me smile. It was so random and specific, and totally opposite of what Joel's friends had advised me to do.

"That's so funny!" I said. "I was considering taking it to Guitar Center."

"No. I'll come take a look at everything. I'm happy to. You have my number?" Marcos asked.

"I'm not sure," I said. "But I know how to you find you."

I felt awkward standing there with him. I didn't know if I should hug him, or if he was going to hug me. I was the recipient of a lot of hugs in those days. Grief hugs, support hugs, awkward hugs.

Marcos reached out and squeezed my arm. "I'll be in touch, OK?" I nodded yes and watched as he climbed back onto the stage to continue with the show.

I got home and just sat in the dark for a while. I thought about Marcos and our conversation. I liked that he and Joel knew each other. I was relieved that he would help with the guitars. But more than my encounter with Marcos, I couldn't help but question, *Is this really my life now?*

I am alone. I am single. I am a widow.

Where is Joel?!

I felt empty and sad. I felt lonely.

Everything felt like too much.

I picked up my phone and scrolled through my messages. I found Allison's voicemail and finally listened to it. I had to give her credit. I don't know that I could call a stranger-widow and offer any comfort.

But I liked what she said, and we had enough people in common. I took a breath and decided to get back to her. It was too late to call so I sent a text.

Hi, it's Melissa Gould. Thanks for your message, and I'm sorry about your husband. Maybe we can meet for coffee one day.

I startled when the dogs started barking.

"Mom?"

Sophie had come home. She put down her things and turned on the lights. "Why are you sitting in the dark?"

"I hadn't noticed. How was rehearsal?" I asked.

"Fun," she said. "But what's for dinner?"

I looked at the clock. It was after ten. "Dinner?! Didn't they order pizza or something?"

"Yeah, but there was none left because we were practicing my solo when it got there."

"OK," I said. "I'll make you something."

I shuffled into the kitchen, tired, confused, as always.

Sophie unpacked her things while I started boiling water for pasta. "How was Marcos's show?"

"It was nice. I saw some of your friends there. And Marcos. He asked about you."

"That's nice."

"It's hard," I said, my voice cracking. "Being out without Daddy. I miss him."

Sophie nodded. I saw her thinking.

"He's not going to see me in my play," she said.

I searched for the right thing to say, when all I wanted to do was collapse on the floor and sob.

Joel won't be here for her play . . .

Or for middle school graduation, which is just a few months away.

He won't be here on her first day of high school.

He won't be here to teach her how to drive in a few years.

He won't be here when she gets her first job.

Or at her wedding.

And he will never meet his grandchildren.

I swallowed down all of those thoughts and sadness and tried to figure out a response.

"I think he'll still see you in the play," I said after a minute. "I'm not sure how. But I know he wouldn't miss it."

She thought about that. Then she said, "You know how when Daddy was in the hospital and I would ask you, *He's going to be OK, right? He's going to be fine?* Well, I think he is. I think he's OK now."

A mountain of love burst through my heart. I approached Sophie to give her a hug. She put up her hands to stop me.

"Don't."

It's not that she was cold or unaffectionate. She was a teenager. Sophie liked having her space, but this behavior was fairly new. I often asked myself, *Is this because she's a teenager or because her dad died?*

So I just stared at her. My beautiful, wise, soulful daughter.

"I think Daddy's OK now, too," I said.

I started to heat up some sauce when my phone beeped with an incoming text.

"Your phone," Sophie said.

"Oh, maybe it's that Allison," I said looking at the clock. "It's late."

"It's Marcos!" she said.

"What?" My stomach jumped the slightest bit. My hands were full so I asked her, "What does it say?"

"Hi, it's Marcos. This is my number. Please let me know a good time to come by. I'm happy to help. Smiles." Sophie looked up at me. "Smiles?"

I shrugged. "I don't know."

"What is he helping with?" It took me a minute to answer as my mind wandered. Why was Marcos texting me? He must have had my number from when he taught Sophie.

"Mom!" Sophie said.

"You know how everyone is always asking to help us? I told him about the guitars and stuff. He's going to help me sort out what to do with all of it," I said.

"Oh," she said. "Cool."

"Yeah," I said. "It is."

Sophie let me kiss the top of her head. I drained the pasta. I added the sauce. Got the parmesan cheese. I put down two bowls. Two forks. Two napkins.

Sophie got us both some water. Although I may have had wine.

I sat down at the counter.

"Come eat, Smoosh."

Sophie sat next to me.

We had a counter in the kitchen that the three of us usually sat at and had all of our meals on. It was large but we only had two barstools for it. One of us always sat on a smaller stool or stood. We hadn't had to pull over the small stool since Joel died. I thought that with every meal.

So Sophie and I sat in the kitchen, eating pasta late on a Friday night. The dogs were in their beds. The house was quiet.

I picked up my phone to look at Marcos's text. Just seeing his name made me smile a little. I asked for help and here he was, offering it.

Smiles, he wrote. *Was that the point?*

If so, it was working.

FOURTEEN

Easy

A re you going to start crying again?" Allison asked as I sipped my cappuccino. I nodded yes as I reached for my napkin to dab my eyes.

"I get it," she said, and then took a bite of her omelet.

This was our first meeting. The Meeting of *The Widows*. We had made a plan via text and here we were, a month after she first reached out and left me a message. Allison and I recognized each other from the neighborhood and hugged upon saying hello.

"I have a feeling that our husbands are also meeting for the first time. Like they're with us. Or at least watching us."

"You think so?" Allison said.

I liked this Allison Frank. She had an easy smile and warm brown eyes and never stopped talking. She told me about Brad, her husband who had died unexpectedly three years ago. It looked like he dropped dead of a heart attack, but an autopsy revealed it was amyloidosis—a disorder where abnormal proteins in your blood can cause life-threatening organ failure. Brad sounded like someone with a great sense of humor. I'm sure Joel and I would have loved him. She told me about her twin teenage daughters, whom I couldn't wait to introduce to Sophie. She told me about her connection to our temple and rabbi. She named some other young*ish* widows and widowers in the neighborhood. But she also told me about the kind of music she liked and what books and movies she recently enjoyed. She told me about her recent travels and where she grew up in Florida, which, coincidentally, is where my grandmother used to live. She told me about cousins of hers who had come to town, and all of the places she took them. She knew a lot about a lot of things. She was a little rough around the edges, extremely down-to-earth, and I felt that even if we didn't have widowhood and "only" parenting in common, we would be friends.

She seemed to have a full life. She had a lot of friends and always had plans. She had figured out how to make a life without her husband.

"I'm open to meeting someone; it just hasn't happened yet."

"I still feel married to Joel," I said.

"I know," she said. "But I doubt he wants you to be alone."

I nodded. Tears started to flow again.

"I don't know how to be with someone who's not him," I admitted.

"You'll have to figure that out, I guess," she said.

"So listen," she said as we were about to leave. "When Brad died, another young widow reached out to me, and it helped. Which is why I reached out to you. So now maybe if you hear of someone whose spouse dies, you'll reach out to them. It's like a little widow hotline."

"I don't know if I'm ready for that," I said. "It took me weeks just to call you back."

"Well, maybe one day you'll feel differently. Or we'll do it together."

"Like a widow club or something?" I said, shaking my head. "It's so sad, it's funny."

I pictured a bat signal in the sky, only it was a sad face emoji, or a skull and crossbones, that would let us know that someone had died and left someone else behind.

"Widows to the rescue!" I said.

"Well," Allison said, smiling, "it's really hard in the beginning. It's nice to talk to someone who has been there."

Friends who had encouraged me to return Allison's call were right. It did help sitting down and talking with another young*ish* widow. I liked hearing about her daughters, and I liked hearing about her openness to dating. It had crossed my mind, too, but then as soon as I'd have the thought, Joel would pop into my mind, and I simply couldn't imagine it.

Who else will I even be attracted to? Who else will I want to open my heart to? Who other than Joel will even come close to understanding me?

I was intrigued by what the psychic had told me about someone new, but I had no idea who she meant. When I'd mention to Ellie that the psychic said there's a new man on the horizon and he's someone I already know, we would laugh over who it might be.

"Maybe it's that taxi driver we met in Vegas. He literally wouldn't take his eyes off of you. Remember? We almost got killed!" she'd say, laughing.

"Yes," I'd say, "but that was a woman, not a man."

"Then maybe it's that doctor of Joel's? The one you'd call Prince Charming?"

Joel had had a doctor on his MS team who literally looked like a prince from a Disney movie. Long dark hair, strong jaw, athletic build.

"He's too young and has no children. The psychic said the new guy has a son," I'd remind her.

"Hmm," Ellie would wonder. "What would Joel do?"

"I don't know," I'd say.

"Joel!" Ellie would say looking toward the sky. "We need you!"

"We do, but let's not bother him with this."

"Oy," she'd say. "This is all too much."

"Way too much," I'd agree.

Life was moving forward without Joel. We lived in the same house. I drove the same car and slept in the same bed, but everything was different. It was confusing. Like being lost in a place that was entirely familiar. It was as if all of a sudden, everyone started speaking a different language . . . Imagine every street sign, every piece of mail, every instruction manual, every song, every conversation was now in another language. You never learned this other language, but since everything else was still the same, you just forged ahead and managed somehow. Then one day, you realized, *Hey, everything is the same, but totally different!* And you had that thought in the new language. That's where I was in the grief process. I was living my life in this new language. I was still learning it, getting the hang of it, but it was sounding more and more familiar.

I noticed that with Allison. Whenever I met another widow or widower (I like to call them *wisters*—widow sisters and widow misters), we spoke the same language. It's based in grief and resilience, a knowing we've been to the same place.

My Spanish friend Maria did Clooney with me one day. She wanted to go off the main path to a different one, a harder climb, the end of which had a waterfall in a lush pasture. I'm sure it was beautiful. I'm sure the extra bit of exercise would have done me good. But as we huffed and puffed our way up the original mountain trail, I said to her, "I don't think I can make it. Not today, but let's do it another time."

"Oh, come on," she pleaded, "you can do it!"

"I know I can, but this is hard enough right now."

She stopped midstride, thoughtful.

"Do you know something?" she said. "You are right. For you, everything is difficult right now. So you know what?" she asked. "You're making the right decision. You need to take it easy. From now on, everything you do, choose easy."

"Easy?" I asked.

"Yes! Every thought, every task, every chore, do whatever is easiest for you," she said. "You lost your husband. What is harder than that?!"

"True," I said.

"I mean it," she said, shaking her index finger. "I think we are onto something with this."

We continued up the hill. I liked the sun on my face, the soft breeze through the trees. It felt peaceful. Maria understood that just living my life every day was difficult because Joel was no longer in it. So the idea of making everything easy struck me as a solution to the weight I felt I had been carrying around since he died. I felt heavy and tired all the time, even when I was doing things I enjoyed. That was grief. But maybe I didn't need to push myself to do the things I found difficult just because I thought I *should* be doing them.

I'd feel guilty using the dishwasher when there were only two of us at home now. But making things easy meant I would use the dishwasher more often. That was easier than washing every plate, fork, and glass that piled up in the sink. It meant alleviating my meal planning stress by accepting that we would eat more frozen pizza and ready-made salads. Easy meant I didn't feel compelled to answer every email and text the minute I received one.

Making things easy meant that I could give myself permission to admit that losing my husband was the hardest thing I'd ever been through, and that I was doing the best I could.

∽

Marcos told me that he had exactly a half an hour to spend looking through our music equipment. We had texted the day before, and I was glad to be moving forward. I got the impression that Marcos was a busy guy. In addition to his music, teaching and playing gigs around town, I knew he was involved with the food pantry and neighborhood church, which is also where he lived and taught music—in a bungalow in the back. A few years earlier, shortly after meeting him and talking about him with some other parents, I thought I knew his whole story.

"Hun," I said to Joel one night when we were getting ready for bed. "I bet Marcos is in Alcoholics Anonymous."

"I don't know," he said, flossing his teeth, not really interested. "Maybe."

"Why else would he be so involved in the church?" I asked. "He runs or helps out with the food pantry, and he lives right there with his son. He was probably some horrible alcoholic or drug addict. He probably has a tattoo."

"What a shock," Joel said, smiling. "You're making up stories."

"But it tracks, don't you think?"

"I haven't really thought about it but, sure." Joel was always so patient with me.

I continued. "He probably hit rock bottom, found Jesus, found the church . . ."

Joel shrugged.

"Found God or whatever and is now devoted to giving back." I was so pleased with myself. "I bet he's, like, a Jesus freak but kind of low-key about it. Makes total sense."

"Yeah," Joel said. "I mean, maybe. I don't know. His girlfriend is an actress or a model or something. I think she lives there with him."

"I didn't know he had a girlfriend," I said, trying to see how she fit into my story. "Hmm, maybe she's an addict, too."

Marcos's life was intriguing. It was so different from mine and Joel's. I wanted to figure it out. Figure *him* out. He seemed grounded and confident. Very masculine. He was a musician. Jesus Lover. Addict. This was the story I had made up about him, and I was sticking to it.

I was feeling good the day Marcos came over. I was looking forward to my writing group that night. I was also happy to be making progress cleaning out the garage. I wasn't just getting rid of Joel's things either. I had boxes of tax returns I was happy to shred and dispose of. I had boxes of scripts from every show I've ever written on. I had yearbooks and articles I wrote for my high school newspaper. I found my child-hood report cards and journals and old photo albums.

I got rid of all of it.

Stuff was just *stuff*. I didn't want to hold on to any of it. This was something that Leigh called *high-level spirituality*. Fine with me.

When Marcos showed up, I had just gotten home from a long walk with the dogs. I was sweaty, my hair was a mess inside one of Joel's baseball caps, and I may not have brushed my teeth yet that morning. I had lined up the guitars and amplifiers in front of the garage. I opened the gate to my driveway when I saw Marcos pull up in his big black Toyota Tundra. I saw him get out of his truck in a red T-shirt and jeans, his mass of thick dark hair slicked back as if he had just gotten out of the shower. He took a sip out of his coffee cup—an actual ceramic mug, not a Starbucks paper cup—and approached with confidence, all business.

"Hey. Good morning. How are you?" he said. But he wasn't looking at me at all. He was eyeing all of the gear. He immediately picked up a guitar for inspection. He strummed it a little bit, tuning it, listening. He smiled and set it down.

"I have a student looking for these," he said about some pedals and a microphone, making a pile.

He moved over to two amplifiers, inspecting them.

"I'm pretty sure this stuff all works. Joel kept everything in such great condition," I said.

"Yeah, I can tell."

I watched him fiddle with cables on the back of the amps as I tried to keep the dogs from barking and running around this stranger.

He finally glanced my direction. "I have a guy in Torrance. He'd take these off your hands." He made another pile, looked at his watch.

"Is any of this worth anything? I mean, I'm happy to donate it but—"

"Oh yeah," he said, "people will pay for this stuff."

"Well," I said, "take whatever you want or need first. I mean, I appreciate your help so . . ."

I felt he should be compensated for his time. He picked up one of Joel's electric guitars. He examined it, played it although it made no sound, not being plugged in.

"This one," Marcos said, smiling. "This one is special. I know where to take it, but you'll probably have to go with me. There might be paperwork."

"Um . . . OK." I didn't understand what I was agreeing to, but fine.

Marcos started carrying some of the lighter gear to his truck. "OK if I take this stuff with me now?"

"Sure," I said.

He seemed hurried. "I'll get back to you, OK? You have some good stuff here. Really."

"OK, great," I said.

"You're going to be fine. Joel did a good job."

I must have made a face. I had no idea what he meant. *Joel did a good job keeping his music gear in good condition?* Or did he mean that *Joel did a good job in life? In choosing me as his wife? With our family?*

Marcos looked back and smiled at me. He laughed a little and reached out, touching my arm. "You're doing good, Melissa. It's going to be OK."

His brown eyes crinkled at the sides, and he looked genuinely happy. I watched him get into his truck.

"I appreciate you coming by," I said as he started the engine and rolled down the window.

"I'll be in touch," he said as he reversed out of my driveway, coffee mug back in hand.

Then he was gone. The whole exchange was so fast. I looked around like, *What just happened?*

I walked up my driveway and saw less than half of what I had pulled out of the garage. I felt a sense of relief. I trusted Marcos to handle it.

But it felt odd. I didn't *think* that he was afraid of *The Widow* . . . but we only discussed the gear, and hardly even that. He was so casual.

He mentioned Joel easily and seemed perfectly comfortable with the task at hand. We didn't know each other well. In fact, we really didn't know each other at all. Sophie hadn't had a lesson with him in over a year, and I had only met him a handful of times at most, including the night I asked for his help. Maybe he was just a no-nonsense guy. An attractive no-nonsense guy. A really cool no-nonsense guy.

I went inside and called Jillian.

"Are you sitting down?" I asked.

"Uh-oh," she said. "What happened?"

"Sophie's guitar teacher, you know, who we saw play the other night? He just came over and took a bunch of Joel's music gear with him."

"OK," she said.

"And it was totally . . ." I tried to come up with the word. "It was like . . . He acted sort of . . . I don't know what I'm trying to say," I admitted.

"Did he hit on you?" she asked.

"Oh my God, no!" I said. "I wish!"

I wasn't expecting that to come out of my mouth.

"Ha!" Jillian laughed.

I gasped. "I can't believe I just said that!"

"You told me you thought he was sexy."

"Sexy? Is that the word I used?" I asked.

"Yup," she said.

Joel had been gone for six months. In that time, a good friend had tried to fix me up with one of his brothers, who was moving back to LA after living abroad most of his adult life. I told him I wasn't ready.

Sophie had a friend whose parents had been divorced since we met them in elementary school. The dad had messaged me early on to tell me that he always liked me, and that if I ever wanted to grab coffee or a drink, to please be in touch. I declined.

I also received a marriage proposal from an English guy I exchanged a few words with in the wine aisle of Trader Joe's. I told him I'd think about it (*he had dimples!*).

The thought of meeting someone new, or even getting together with someone I already knew, was not appealing. I was a married woman. I was married to a man I loved. It was baffling to even consider dating because, how could I? I loved Joel. My marriage didn't *feel* like it was over, even though it was. But not by choice.

Marcos and I were Facebook friends, probably from when he first started teaching Sophie. I scoured his page, looking for clues to his personal life. There was nothing about a wife and nothing about a model girlfriend either. Nor did I see anything about his son. What I did see was post after post about his past and upcoming gigs. Where most people I knew were bragging about their kids' accomplishments, or posting silly pet photos, or getting into deep discussions about neighborhood issues, Marcos seemed to live in a world of self-promotion. I got it. He was making a living as a musician. He kept things professional.

A few years earlier, Joel had come home from one of Sophie's guitar lessons. I was in the office writing. Joel walked in, kissed me hello, and handed me a CD.

I looked at it. "What's this?"

"Marcos's newest CD. You should listen to it. I think you'll like it."

I shrugged and put it near my car keys so I could listen to it in the car. I always took Joel's music recommendations to heart. Marcos's sound was bluesy and skilled—I liked it.

Now I was mourning my husband and tried to practice what I always preached to Sophie: *Just feel your feelings, whatever they may be.* Grief was my constant companion who occasionally took naps. It was during those nap times that I made my way back to myself. Through my writing. Through my spiritual readings. Through my close friendships. And now, through the slight rumblings of attraction to someone new.

It was easier than I care to admit, to consider a possible fling. But it was also unrealistic. I had no idea what Marcos's personal life was, other than what I assumed was a clean and sober existence. Plus, as confident and casual as he seemed, I was a widow. Who'd want to deal with that kind of complication?

Over the course of a couple of weeks, I heard from Marcos about some of the music gear that he was able to sell or donate.

Sold the acoustic, the text would read. Or, Keeping the harmonica for my lessons. Smiles. Once, I came home and there was an envelope under my front door mat with some cash in it. A Post-it note inside said, *From Marcos.*

It was a weird way of doing business, but taking Maria's advice, I decided to keep things easy and tried not to think about it too much.

One night, Sophie lying next to me in bed, I got a text from Marcos asking if I was available to go to the guitar shop with him the next day to try to sell Joel's one remaining guitar. My stomach did a flip-flop. I was excited. I was nervous. And I felt guilty about the kind of thoughts I was allowing myself to entertain.

It's nothing. A simple business transaction. As Joel liked to remind me, I was a writer. I was creating a scenario between Marcos and me that didn't make sense. I was a Jew*ish* only parent and widow who was trying to get back to living my life. He was a recovering drug addict and/or alcoholic who lived behind a church, taught and played music, and fed the homeless.

These were the thoughts I had as I fell asleep that night. They were a welcome reprieve.

FIFTEEN

Marcos

When the waiter came by for our lunch order, I asked for the two-enchilada combo plate with rice and beans.

"Anything to drink?" he asked.

I shook my head no and ran my fingers through my hair. It had been up and under a baseball cap when Marcos picked me up to go to the guitar store. I hadn't slept well the night before, and in the morning I was in the usual rush getting Sophie out the door. I walked the dogs and did some work for Joel's company but hadn't had time to shower.

"Ready?" he asked when I opened the door that morning.

"Yes, thanks for picking me up," I said.

"No problem." He opened the truck door so I could climb in.

I was a mess. I felt frazzled, nervous. Marcos was calm as ever. Steady. I thought it might be awkward driving with him, but it wasn't. He was sporting his usual jeans and T-shirt attire. His hair was thick, and his beard the solid five o'clock shadow it always was.

"So I think the guy's name is George. He owns the store, and he said he'd take the guitar on consignment. You'll get your money but it could be a few months. Or maybe only a day, depends who swings by."

"Sounds good," I said. "I'm in no rush."

"Good," Marcos said. "And this gives me an excuse to go into his shop. It's for serious musicians. You'll see."

He smiled at me. I felt my face turn red, and so I looked out the window instead. It felt like someone else's life. Someone young, inexperienced, and carefree. Not someone who watched her husband suffer through a horrible illness and ultimately die of a mosquito bite. Not someone who slept with her fourteen-year-old daughter every night because they were both afraid of being alone.

I handled the business transaction with George while Marcos acted like a kid in a candy store. He plugged in every guitar that interested him and played with genuine abandon.

I sat down and observed him going from one guitar to the next, talking shop with the owner and his assistant. He winked at me as he crossed my path, headed for another guitar.

"Real serious musicians," I said.

He stopped and smiled. "I'm sorry. You're probably bored to death."

"Not at all!" I said. I wasn't. This wasn't my world. It was nice feeling incognito.

He noticed as I checked my phone for the time.

"We'll get out of here, soon. What time are you picking up Sophie?"

It startled me when he mentioned Sophie. My real life seemed so far away.

"Not for a couple of hours," I said.

"Good," he said, smiling.

We ended up at the Mexican restaurant down the street. Our eyes had to adjust to the dim lighting as we were shown to a quiet booth. My inner voice was telling me this wasn't a date (but it felt like one) and was also trying to tell me that I looked good (I didn't) and to remember everything so that I could tell Jillian about it later. Mariachi music played softly on the speakers behind us; I was impressed as Marcos ordered his lunch in broken Spanish.

"*Señor, por favor,*" he said to the waiter. "*Un chile relleno*, one *enchilada de pollo*, and *un taco de pollo.*"

I figured Marcos had some Hispanic origins, but it didn't occur to me that he could actually speak Spanish. I was riveted.

"Anything to drink?" the waiter asked him.

Marcos looked to me. "You're sure you don't want anything?"

"I'm good," I said.

"OK." Marcos turned to the waiter. "I'll just have a beer, please. *Una cerveza.* Thank you."

My heart started pounding. Hard. *Did Marcos just order a beer?*

The waiter smiled and walked away. I looked at Marcos.

"Are you sure you can do that?"

He raised his eyebrows. "Do what?"

"Have a beer?" I said.

"Well, yeah. I'm not teaching until tonight, so . . ."

I quietly panicked. Marcos was falling off the wagon right in front of me, and I didn't know what to do. I reached for my phone. I wanted to call Joel. *Hun, Marcos just ordered a beer! What should I do?* I sat deflated, confused. I felt like crying.

"What's the matter?" Marcos looked at me.

"I just . . . I thought you didn't drink," I said.

He smiled. "Well, I do. Every now and then. I like a beer with my Mexican food." A concerned look came over his face. "I mean, if drinking is a problem for you—" He started to signal the waiter. I stopped him.

"No, no. It's fine. I drink. I like to."

He settled in and started eating some chips and salsa. The conversation could have gone in many directions. We were two people, two adults, having lunch together in a Mexican restaurant in our shared neighborhood. But the conversation taking place in my mind was so loud—*Joel, you're not going to believe it!*—that I had to excuse myself from the table. I went to the bathroom.

I got the story wrong, all wrong! I can't trust myself, I thought.

I didn't mind that Marcos was drinking, in fact I was relieved in a way. But if I got his backstory wrong and the narrative that I had created about him, then what else might I misinterpret? I didn't know him at all, which made me even more nervous. How could I dare to determine if this was a date or just an extension of our business transaction? I wanted to call Joel so badly that I started praying. *Tell me what to do, hun . . . I don't know what this is! . . . Marcos is not who I thought he was, who we thought he was!*

I stared at myself in the mirror, ran some cold water on my inner wrists, and breathed.

When I got back to the table, Marcos's beer had arrived. I picked it up and drank half of it in one giant gulp. He gave me a look.

"Sorry," I said.

"You OK?" he asked. "You seem a little . . . I don't know, nervous or something."

"I'm sorry," I said. "It's just. Well, it's a lot. And I thought, I mean, Joel and I thought, that maybe you were in AA?"

He started laughing.

"Joel thought that? Why?"

"Well, I mean, I may have convinced him of it. I just thought . . . You do some work with the food pantry, right?"

"I'm the director. Going on six years."

"You're the director of the whole food pantry? Do you get paid for that?" I couldn't help but be direct.

"Nope. Strictly volunteer."

"Wow," I said. "You must meet a lot of homeless people."

He nodded his head, ran a hand through his thick hair. I could tell he was considering a response.

"The pantry isn't just for the homeless. There's a lot of elderly people. A mom or a dad who just lost a job or who've been out of work. People who fall just below the poverty line."

"So why do you do it? Especially if it's volunteer," I asked.

Marcos started to laugh.

"Why? Well, it's the kind of thing, I guess you could say . . ." He really was contemplating the question. "I guess I think that if I don't do it, who will?"

The people I knew wrote checks. Maybe volunteered once a year at Thanksgiving or Christmas by feeding people in homeless shelters. I had never seen or heard of real-life altruism like this.

Marcos looked at me, his eyes slightly squinted, like he was trying to figure me out.

"So why do you think I'm an alcoholic?" he asked.

I tried to tread lightly.

"Well. You live at the church, right?"

He nodded.

"They have AA meetings there . . . and you're raising your son there—"

The minute I said *son* I had to catch my breath. The psychic. She said a man who has a son, someone I already know, loves me. *Will love me. Future love me. Marcos?*

"You ever meet Davis? He's just a couple of years older than Sophie. She knows him."

The truth is, everyone in our neighborhood knew Davis. He was the quintessential bad boy. Wild. Gorgeous. Troubled. Girls who were scared of him also had crushes on him. Boys who *weren't* scared of him wanted to be his friend.

"OK, I'm just going to say it. I thought that since you lived at the church and worked at the pantry, you must be in recovery. Found Jesus. And devoted your life to giving back out of gratitude for being saved. Like, maybe you were a born-again Christian or something?"

I couldn't help myself and added, "Or . . . maybe you were a drug addict?"

"What? No!"

I covered my mouth with my hand. I was slightly mortified by my assumptions.

"I'm sorry!" I muttered. Then, because I couldn't help myself: "Any tattoos?"

Marcos started laughing, shaking his head. "Wow," he said. "You're a writer, right? Did you tell me that or did Joel?"

"I don't know if I did," I said, liking that he mentioned Joel again.

"Your husband must have told me. You're good. That's a story, alright," he said. "It's all wrong. Not even close, but plausible. Points for plausible."

We both smiled as our food arrived. I had taken Marcos's beer. The waiter asked if he wanted another. He considered for a minute, then shook his head, smiling. "No, thank you, *compadre*. Better not."

The beer helped calm my nerves. I gobbled up my cheese enchiladas. They were delicious. Marcos and I talked easily, but I couldn't help but feel like he was doing me a favor. Yes, he had helped with Joel's guitars, which I was grateful for. But it felt like he was taking out his friend's kid sister on the night of the prom to distract her from the fact that she didn't get asked to go.

When he dropped me off at home, he got out of his truck and came around to open my door. He then got back in on the driver's side, said, "I'll be in touch," and drove off.

When I picked up Sophie from school that afternoon, she got in the car and asked, "What's for dinner?"

It was always the first thing she asked when I picked her up. There could have been an earthquake that morning, there could have been a horse in the back seat, I could have even been driving a different car, but no matter what, this was the first and usually only question she ever asked.

"Cheese enchiladas," I told her.

"Yay!" She clapped happily.

Thankfully she didn't ask where I had gotten them. I didn't want to tell her about my afternoon with Marcos. It would be too confusing and too weird to tell her that he and I had lunch, so I didn't volunteer the information either. We were both just happy she had something delicious for dinner that night.

The following week, as I was pulling up to my writing group, my phone rang. I checked to make sure it wasn't Sophie, and instead I saw Marcos's name pop up.

"Hello?" I answered.

"Melissa! It's Marcos," he said. He sounded happy. "So listen. I realized you asked me a question the other day that I didn't answer."

I did a quick inventory of my inquisition. AA, check. Drugs, check. Do-gooder, check. *So what's my unanswered question?*

"Oh-kay," I said. Now I was smiling.

"Do you remember what it was you asked me?"

"Um . . . not specifically."

"Well the answer is no, I don't have any tattoos," he said.

My face almost hurt from smiling. "Ha, well, that's . . ." I couldn't think of what to say.

"Are you surprised?" he asked.

"That I got everything I thought I knew about you wrong? Yes, that's a surprise."

"It's kind of funny," he said. "That you were thinking about me at all."

"Well." I tried to cover. "I put some thought into who spends time with my daughter, so . . ."

"You're a good mom, Melissa. Joel was a good father. Sophie's lucky."

"Really? Her dad just died, so I don't know how lucky that makes her," I said, cringing at what had just come out of my mouth.

"Well yeah, yes. That's . . . It's just sad. But she'll be OK. She knows that both her parents loved her," he said.

"Thank you. Thanks for saying that, for recognizing that." I noticed the time. My class was starting soon.

"So were you just calling to tell me about the tattoos?" I asked.

"I thought maybe we could get a drink one night. If you're OK with that. Casual, easy. No problem."

I noticed the awkwardness of his phrasing, but it didn't bother me.

"Yes," I said. "That would be nice."

"Good," he said. "Looking forward to it."

We hung up, and I got out of my car. I fumbled to find my car keys to lock the doors. I was excited and nervous. And while I was also happy, I had to hold back tears. *I miss Joel.* Most of my memories were still of him in the hospital. I got in the habit of looking at pictures of him to remind me that he wasn't always in a coma, that he once lived a life. A life where he wasn't compromised by disease. A life that was full and for the most part, happy.

I had become obsessed with one particular photo. In it, Joel takes up the whole frame and he is smiling and looking down because five-year-old Sophie was the photographer. Joel has a sincere smile, and there's so much love in his face. It's because, I'm convinced, he's staring into his daughter's eyes. She was able to capture that moment in a way that is authentic to their relationship. That is the Joel I wanted to remember. That is the Joel who wouldn't want his young*ish* wife to continue suffering where and when his life left off. That is the Joel who exudes love.

Joel Osteen has a sermon in which he speaks of there being a *season* of mourning as opposed to a *lifetime* of mourning. That resonated for me. I could see where losing Joel could also cost me my livelihood. I wanted to get to the other side of grief, not stay in it forever.

It had been over six months since Joel had died. I didn't know if I was ready to move on with someone new. Not that I was really moving on with anyone. I didn't think I could let myself do that yet. But I did know that my feelings were stirred up a bit. I was ready for . . . something.

SIXTEEN

Man of My Dreams

I f it's OK with you, I'm going to give you a kiss," Marcos said, leaning toward me in the front seat of my car. He smiled, waiting for my consent. He had shaved, and for the first time I noticed he had dimples. I was a sucker for a good dimple. I leaned toward him and as our lips touched, the floor fell out from under me. I felt light as air, which was unnerving—I had felt so heavy since Joel died. It felt like Marcos and I were wrapped in bubbles, weightless and buoyant.

We never made it to drinks. Here's why:

I was terrified.

Unlike our impromptu lunch, this was unequivocally a date. I lacked grown-up dating experience. I lacked confidence. I was still married to the man I loved even though he died.

"Yes, do it!" Jillian said when I called her the next day to tell her that Marcos had asked me out.

"I'm scared, though," I admitted.

"That's OK. This will be good for you. It will be great, no matter what happens."

I wanted to tell all of my friends. And my sister! And the mailman! But I kept it to myself because first and foremost, I didn't want Sophie to know, and I didn't want anyone to accidentally let the information slip. I had already made up my mind that no matter who I dated (because I thought that I would *eventually*), I wouldn't tell Sophie about it unless it was serious because, why would I? It wouldn't be worth the stress and upset it would cause.

Going out "for a drink" had me feeling self-conscious, too. I was afraid we'd run into someone I knew, and they'd be suspicious or judgy or overly excited. So to avoid all of these things—we agreed that we would meet at a restaurant with a full bar, at 2:00 p.m. On a Wednesday. I couldn't make plans for an evening because I was still building my schedule around Sophie's.

I also insisted that we meet in downtown Burbank. It was close but not so close that we would risk running into anyone familiar. I hoped.

Lastly, I suggested that we drive separately. But with all of my planning for what was starting to feel like an illicit affair, I did not count on seeing Marcos standing outside the restaurant by the valet parking area. We agreed we would meet inside, at the bar. I had the irrational thought that *he must be canceling*. I rolled down my window. He smiled and said, "Best-laid plans. They don't open until dinner. Three more hours."

I exhaled, relieved that he wasn't backing out, but seeing him standing there, talking to me through the open window, made me panic.

"Get in!" I ordered. Marcos got in the passenger seat. "I don't want anyone to see us!" I said as I sped down the street toward the residential area.

Marcos started laughing. "What's happening? Where are you taking me?"

I pulled over, my hands gripping the steering wheel. My mind was racing. *This is crazy! I'm crazy! What am I doing? My husband just died! Joel . . . Joel . . . Where are you? Is this OK? That I'm with Marcos? Oh my*

God! I'm a bad person, I thought. *I'm a bad wife and a bad mother, and I shouldn't be here!*

I looked at Marcos. I had tears in my eyes. He nodded, patiently.

"You know," he said. "It's OK. Whatever you're thinking. Whatever's going through your head right now? I'll just sit right here."

He was killing me. *Who is this man? This church-living, feed-the-homeless musician/teacher/do-gooder?*

"I'm sorry," I said. "I feel like I'm making this into such a big deal, and it's just a drink. I mean it's nothing; this is nothing! And now we're not even getting a drink! I'm just a little nervous about all this. Maybe it's too soon, or too much?"

Marcos looked at me. He appeared comfortable sitting there. Like he didn't have a care in the world. "I mean . . ." He tried to find some words but after a minute, he just shrugged. I felt a need and desire to touch him, so I did. I gently placed my hand on his arm.

"It's just, I love Joel. He's my husband, and we're still married."

"I get that," Marcos said.

"How do you get that?" I asked. "Does it even make sense? It sounds crazy but also, not crazy. I think I'm going crazy."

Marcos looked into my eyes. "Look. I think it's all pretty normal. I think you've been through a lot. You and Joel were solid. You were."

I nodded. He was making sense. My mind may have been slowing down but my heart was still racing.

"I think you have a lot going on, especially up here." He tapped his temple, then reached over and tapped mine. I smiled. "So I'm thinking that maybe you need to just relax a little bit. Does that sound OK? Like you just need to . . . relax."

"Yes, I think you're right," I said, considering how exactly to do that.

"So," he said, "if it's OK with you, I'm going to give you a kiss. I think that might help."

He leaned toward me, and I let him kiss me. It was soft and tender and exactly what I needed to calm down. I kissed him back. We stayed like that, kissing in the front seat of my Toyota Prius for over an hour. It was a good, old-fashioned make-out session that as a married woman of over sixteen years, I hadn't experienced in quite a while.

If I didn't see Marcos again after that day, it would be OK because that particular moment was so excruciatingly perfect, it would forever be enough. It was exactly what I needed. While I had experienced some levity and happiness in the aftermath of Joel's death, this was a feeling that managed to touch a part of me I forgot existed.

It was *desire*.

I wanted this to happen; I had wished for this to happen. Marcos fulfilled that desire. It was everything.

"I'd like to see you again," he said when we parted. We both seemed drunk with kisses, silly smiles on our faces.

"Me, too."

He went through his weekly schedule, counting off each task on a finger. "I'm teaching most of tomorrow into tomorrow night and the next day. I also have to be at the hospital in the afternoon. I have a board meeting this week, and I'll be at the pantry Friday and Monday. I have a gig next—"

"Wait." I stopped him. "What hospital?" *Is he sick? Dying? Or just visiting a friend?*

"The children's hospital. I go once a month."

I gave him a look. "Why?"

"I volunteer," he said. "I bring my guitar and sing to the kids."

"What kids?" I asked.

"The sick and dying children."

My mouth must have dropped open.

"For real?"

"It's meaningful work. The families appreciate it. I like doing it. Going on almost ten years."

"So, wait," I said. "In addition to running the food pantry, you also volunteer at the children's hospital? So you can sing to the dying children?"

My mind flashed to the ICU where Joel spent the last weeks of his life. I couldn't imagine a musician coming in to perform in those corridors. But the nurses and doctors and entire ICU staff appreciated Joel's music playlist that flowed out of the small portable speakers I brought over. So I got it . . . sort of.

"So anyway, got a full schedule these next few weeks, but I want to make sure you're in it. Sound good?"

I nodded . . . confused. . . smitten . . . interested. *Is Marcos a modern-day Jesus? Is he the Devil?* I had no idea. But I knew I wanted more of him.

~

At night, when I was going to sleep, I would pray for Joel to come visit me. I missed him so much. I had so much to tell him.

I had a dream once that was so real and vivid, it brings me to tears every time I think about it. In our neighborhood, there is a main road that connects via a bridge. Most drivers don't even realize they're driving over a bridge because the body of water it covers is a thin, mostly concrete section of the Los Angeles River that serves as an overflow space for when it rains. When you walk across the bridge, however, you realize that you're walking from one side of town into the other. You're "crossing over."

In my dream, I was on the north side of the bridge walking south. The sun was shining. It was a beautiful and clear day. I looked up and walking toward me on the other side of the bridge, waving wildly with the biggest smile I had ever seen, was Joel. I couldn't believe my eyes! *There he is!* My love, my everything. It took my breath away to see him like that—*so alive! So healthy!* I couldn't move. I couldn't believe it was him! I smiled and started to wave back. I called out his name, *Joel!* I kept thinking, *He's so happy! And he's right there; he's RIGHT THERE!*

He continued to wave with his entire arm. Broad, wide air strokes with that big smile. It was so real. *He is so close. He is real! He is alive!* My heart was going to burst from happiness and also, confusion.

But you died! I rationalized in my sleep.

And the minute I had this thought, I woke up.

It was so cruel. But it was also encouraging. I saw Joel. *He was there.* He was happy and excited. *He saw me!* He was working so hard on his end to prove that he was there. I felt like he had not only heard my prayers—*Come see me in my sleep, hun. Please?!*—but also answered them. It was a gift.

"Daddy was in my dream last night," I told Sophie when she woke up that morning. "It was so real. He was alive—" I started to cry. She cupped her elegant hand on my cheek.

"I'm sorry you always see me crying," I said, sniffling.

"I don't mind," she said. I kissed her hand and squeezed it.

"I forgot to tell you," she said, stretching awake. "I saw a hummingbird yesterday."

One of the gifts we got Joel for his fiftieth birthday was a hummingbird feeder. It was a plain glass cylinder that could be filled with liquid food, and it had a red ledge for the birds to perch on while feeding. Joel loved it. He loved nature and hummingbirds in particular. The red color supposedly attracts hummingbirds, and Joel hung it in our backyard within minutes of receiving it. He never got to enjoy it as much as Sophie and I do. We still have it, and it has seen more hummingbirds than I ever thought lived in all of Los Angeles. Every time Sophie and I see one, no matter where in the world we might be, we believe that it either *is* Joel, or that Joel sent it to us to say hi.

When Joel died, every little scribble he left behind and all of his love notes to us became frame-worthy. Every silly doodle and sketch, whether on cheap refrigerator stationery left in our mailbox by a realtor or the bottom corner of a take-out menu, became proof that Joel lived, that he was here, that we shared our lives with each other.

Somehow, my life was moving forward without him.

With multiple unsuccessful attempts at planning our next drinks date, Marcos and I decided to meet one morning for coffee. I suggested Starbucks.

"It's the one that's right on the boulevard, across the street from the Gap," I said. "Know which one I mean?"

"Um, no actually," he replied.

"Really? It's the Starbucks on the boulevard, near the CVS?"

He had no idea. We lived one mile from each other, but in totally different worlds.

That is how we came to have coffee at his house. Marcos lived a block from Sophie's school, and while I continued to be a nervous wreck—*Someone may see me standing at your door!*—it was a nice surprise to find that he made excellent coffee.

What I thought (and hoped) might be a lust-filled morning romp was instead time spent getting to know each other because his son was asleep in the next room.

Marcos had recently taken Davis out of his conventional high school and enrolled him in a nontraditional high school with a flexible schedule, with most of the actual schoolwork being done at home. So while I felt free and unencumbered while Sophie was in school during the day, Davis's classroom was Marcos's kitchen table, where we sat between drinking our strong morning coffee and having furtive make-out sessions on the couch.

We continued to meet at his place for a few mornings and got to know each other in an old-fashioned kind of way—by talking. Over coffee. I learned that his father was born and raised in Peru and that Marcos spent his childhood summers in South America with his grandparents. I learned that he had been married before, but not to his son's mother. I learned that bass, not guitar, was his first instrument and that he had students as young as five and older than either one of us.

I still had only told Jillian about him. "I don't get it. You haven't slept with him yet?" she'd say. My answer was we couldn't find the time or place.

We were adults, planning and sneaking around so that our kids wouldn't find out. Our schedules didn't align because Marcos often worked nights—teaching or performing—and as always, I wanted to be available for Sophie.

I met Davis awkwardly one morning when we were both walking into Marcos's house. Me from morning drop-off, Davis from a night out. He gave me the once over, and later Marcos told me that Davis liked me on sight because I didn't *look like* I'd *be moving in anytime soon*.

While I had been in a committed relationship with Joel since I was in my twenties, Marcos had had many relationships. *Many.* Mostly with beautiful actresses and/or models, like Davis's mother. She and Marcos were never married, although they did live together for years. They split up when Davis was a toddler, and while Davis had a relationship with his mother, Marcos was the one who was raising him during his teenage years.

I wasn't looking to be in a relationship. I thought that whatever happened between us would be a fling, at most. I didn't have time for much more than that; neither did he. Our make-out sessions reminded me that mutual desire overrides things like self-consciousness over an aging body and worry if he would ever call me again. I was a widow. I was in my forties. I had already lost everything there was to lose.

I got a text one morning while I was at Clooney.

Come over. Now. It was from Marcos.

All clear? I wrote back.

Yes! he said.

I had never finished Clooney so fast in my life. It didn't matter that I was sweaty when I got to Marcos. Davis would be gone all day and this was our chance.

Marcos answered the door naked. Absolutely nude. With a big smile.

"Welcome!" he said.

Maybe it wasn't romantic, but I found it very funny. And sort of charming. I, too, was naked by the time we got back to his bedroom.

This was not how I pictured our first tryst. Or my first tryst with someone other than Joel. I thought it would be at night, first of all. I thought I may have a buzz going from a romantic dinner date, with wine, that preceded nudity. But then again, all my expectations about Marcos were wrong from the start.

I liked that he knew Joel. He often mentioned him in conversation. He didn't seem scared or daunted or even nervous around *The Widow*. He saw me as a whole person, and just as I found him interesting, he was interested in me. Whatever was happening between us felt different, for both of us.

I loved how he kissed me. I was comforted by the weight of his body next to mine.

Afterward I admitted to him, "You know, I was actually surprised you called me that day. About the tattoos." I started to laugh.

"You're the one who asked me if I had any!" Marcos said.

"Yeah, like a week earlier!"

Marcos smiled.

"I didn't think you were interested," I said.

"Well, your husband had just died. I was proceeding with caution."

"Yeah," I said and sighed.

Joel.

Tears came to my eyes. Marcos squeezed me. I lay there with Marcos but was thinking about Joel. *Are you OK with this, hun? Are you mad at me? If so, can you forgive me?*

"It's alright. You're going to be OK," Marcos said.

I wiped my tears from my face and cried quietly into his arms. He didn't seem to mind.

I inhaled him in and it soothed me. He smelled masculine. His hands and arms were strong from playing guitar every day. I loved how smooth his skin felt and how his hair curled under at the base of his neck. I dried my tears on his chest.

"I'm here," he said, squeezing my shoulder. "I'm right here." He kissed the top of my head.

Wherever this man is, I thought, *is where I want to be.*

SEVENTEEN

Every Everything

I continued with my healing rituals every night (read a passage from *Healing After Loss*, shared a memory of Joel with Sophie, watched my *Real Housewives*, read Iyanla, listened to the Other Joel . . .) and still cried my way through a lot of my days. But I was also in joyful anticipation of meeting up with Marcos, which was about once a week.

Where I seemed so confused in other aspects of my life, with Marcos things were crystal clear. My needs, which were surprisingly physical, were getting met, and neither of us had an issue with that. I never worried that he was overstepping or taking advantage of my vulnerability because we were on the same page. It was a casual fling.

We would meet at his place when the coast was clear, and about an hour later, I'd be home. Our time together was tender, but when we were done there was no pretense that we would spend the rest of the day or night together. Every so often we'd have coffee and talk and laugh in his kitchen. We tried a few times to meet for a drink or go on a "real" date, but it never worked out. We were getting to know each other in spurts—but in an effort to keep things easy, I didn't overthink it. I also didn't think a relationship was necessarily in the cards. I didn't always follow what he was saying, but I liked his company.

Marcos thought like an artist, always just a few inches off the ground, his mind in other places. He was a fierce blues musician but wasn't familiar with bands I loved, like Wilco and the Avett Brothers. He was only aware of pop music because his students would come in wanting to learn the latest Taylor Swift or One Direction song, but otherwise he knew nothing of pop culture. He didn't even own a TV.

He had no idea who the real housewives were, had never seen an episode of *Game of Thrones*, and once referred to Kourtney Kardashian, who he saw in our neighborhood one afternoon, as *some girl who had a bunch of paparazzi following her around when all I wanted to do was get a cup of coffee.*

He loved talking about movies from any genre and era and believed that his film tidbits and comments were common knowledge. He would also refer to actors and directors by their last names.

When I mentioned that I had seen Juliette Lewis at the gas station, he commented that her father was a character actor frequently seen in "Eastwood movies," but he didn't know that she was rumored to be a Scientologist, which to me was far more interesting.

Marcos was hard to follow at times, and he seemed to say things that didn't necessarily pertain to anything he and I would be discussing. If I read him something from the novel I was working on, and I told him that my writing group seemed to like it, he would offer, "If everyone is thinking alike, then somebody isn't thinking."

"Huh?" I'd say.

"Patton. Famous saying of his. Just read his biography."

Our trysts were brief, but meaningful. It was hard to leave him sometimes, and regardless of our differences, our connection felt magnetic. But he always had a student about to show up, or a board meeting to attend, or a gig to get to. And I always had something that needed to get done. I was an only parent now. I was responsible for everything. *Everything.*

In between the work I was doing for Joel's company and my writing, I walked the dogs, took the trash bins in and out, changed the lightbulbs. I did all the driving, and shopping, and laundry. I found tutors and doctors and attended parent-teacher conferences alone because I had no choice. I made sure the grandparents—*all four sets!*—received their birthday cards on time and phone calls from their granddaughter. I made appointments with the electrician to fix the backyard lights, and the painter about the fence repair, and the tree trimmer when a huge tree branch fell down and cracked our driveway. I attended school board meetings and community meetings, and took the dogs to the vet, and planned every breakfast, lunch, snack, and dinner. I cancelled subscriptions, made sure we had health coverage, tried to get some writing jobs. I made sure the car was clean and had gas in the tank and air in the tires. I changed the batteries in the smoke detectors, usually in the middle of the night because that's when they would unnervingly beep. I had to manage when the air conditioner needed repair and when the washing machine wouldn't spin. When we found a giant bug in the house. When one of the dogs got sprayed by a skunk. When the refrigerator started leaking. And every thought, feeling, emotional outburst, and mood, both mine and Sophie's, were mine to manage.

I ordered copies of death certificates and birth certificates and marriage licenses and was put on hold for hours and transferred from department to department every time I changed a utility bill from Joel's name to mine and had to explain *every single time* that the reason for the transfer was because my husband had died.

I was responsible for *every* everything, and I cherished my time with Marcos, because when I was with him, it was a reprieve from the *every*.

While I was Responsible Mom, I also wanted to be Fun Mom, but Sophie's idea of fun was shopping, something I can't bear. I would feel so old, taking her to the mall and not being able to tolerate the loud music in Forever 21. I'd last two minutes; she could last two hours.

She liked getting manicures, me not so much.

"Come on, let's get our nails done together. It will be nice," she'd say on a Sunday morning.

"Total waste of money," I'd counter. "The nail polish will start chipping the minute you dig into your backpack for your notebook."

"Fine!" she'd say, crossing her arms.

"What if we do Clooney?" I'd suggest.

"I don't like hiking," she'd say, considering. "I'd go horseback riding!"

"Horseback riding?! No. You know I'm not an animal person."

"Bowling?" she'd ask. I'd roll my eyes.

We'd go back and forth like this all the time, until one of us would give in, usually me, and we'd end up either back at the mall or out to dinner somewhere.

I wanted to give her the world. I had Joel for twenty-five years; she only had him for thirteen and a half. *She deserves everything and anything she wants.* But then I'd hear Joel's voice telling me, *You're spoiling her, hun.* If I was, I couldn't help it. Sophie didn't act spoiled, because like Joel, she was good to her core.

Her middle school graduation was upon us. Tickets were limited. I couldn't accommodate all of the grandparents, or Jillian, who also wanted to be there. I wanted Sophie to have a father's presence, so I invited Hal to sit with me in the audience.

It was hard to smile through the ceremony when Joel's absence was felt so overwhelmingly. I could picture him there, sitting right next to me in the folding chairs on that warm summer morning on the PE field, balloons adorning the stage. Joel would have stood up, elated, applauding wildly as Sophie's name was called to receive her diploma. He'd look over at me, a tear in his eyes, saying, *She did it, hun! Look at our beautiful girl!* And afterward, he would have given her flowers and posed for pictures with her, never taking his eyes off her, proud dad that he was.

I don't know how Sophie did it. How she walked across the field in her sweet summer dress, diploma in hand, big smile on her face, while everyone in attendance knew her as "the girl whose father died." I kept waiting for her to break down or have a tantrum that year; it never came.

Earlier in the year, I had decided to take her to Paris as a graduation present. Sophie wouldn't be going to summer camp that summer, so the cost of a trip to Paris felt justified. Plus, I had a free airline ticket and enough points to cover most of the cost of our hotel. Hal gave us a ride to the airport, and fifteen hours later, we were wheels down in Paris, France.

We had a full itinerary with a walking tour of the entire city one day, a bike ride excursion in Versailles on another. A close friend from London was coming in for the day to explore the Jardin des Tuileries and Musée de l'Orangerie with us and make quick stops at the Galeries Lafayette and Le Bon Marché. Another friend of mine from our neighborhood was also in Paris with her teenage daughter, and we met up with them a few times for dinner. If it sounds wonderful and *ooh la la*, it was. We were comfortable in Paris, even though we didn't speak the language and it rained almost every day. We ate crepes and ice cream in the shape of roses. We walked almost everywhere and saw the Eiffel Tower, Notre-Dame Cathedral, and the Arc de Triomphe.

But oftentimes, Sophie was moody and tired and wanted to go back to our hotel. She took comfort in her laptop where she could get on Wi-Fi and watch her shows and get on social media. At times it seemed that the only reason she wanted so many photos was so that she could post them, rather than take in the fact that *we were in Paris!* I tried to be patient, but I got annoyed, and we argued.

"We've seen enough!" she'd yell at me when I'd suggest we hit another landmark after a full day. "I don't need to explore the entire city. I want to go back to the hotel!"

I felt in over my head with her emotions. I couldn't keep up with her unpredictable moods. I'd carry food with me at all times, thinking that maybe she had low blood sugar. When she seemed content, I'd relax. When she seemed anxious or disinterested, I acted over-the-top to compensate. It wasn't different because we were in Paris. In general, I wanted to protect her from any kind of upset, but I also wanted her to *feel her feelings*. She seemed angry at me and frustrated, while I felt like I was giving her everything I had to give.

I second-guessed my motives for traveling; maybe it would have been better to stay home, keep up our routine, *get used to life without Joel*. Was I projecting my own feelings and anxiety on to Sophie about being an only parent or was this typical teenage behavior? I checked in with her therapist many times and was assured that Sophie was doing fine, but these behavioral changes still concerned me.

I usually didn't take my phone with us while we were out during the day, so I'd check my email and any messages when we got back to the hotel. I had promised Sophie that we would go back to the Eiffel Tower on our last night so that we could take some photos of it all lit up. But after another full day of exploring and eating, I was surprised to find that my phone was maxed out with messages from home. Our beloved Lucy was sick. She had seemed lethargic and down in recent weeks, and taking her to the vet was on my to-do list for when we returned. But my neighbor Roxanne was trying to reach me. Lucy had stopped eating. She couldn't get up on her hind legs. Roxanne took Lucy to the vet, who said that Lucy was suffering. She was fifteen years old, and it was simply her time. It was true that Lucy was an older dog, but her heart, like mine and Sophie's, was broken. She was confused as to why Joel suddenly disappeared. She didn't seem to recover from losing him eight months ago.

Once again, I was faced with a decision. They could have given Lucy medication to keep her comfortable, but we wouldn't be home for eight more days. I couldn't bear to have her in so much distress for that long.

I called my mom, and she met Roxanne at the vet. She and Roxanne were there to comfort Lucy as she took her last breath. Sophie and I cried and hugged each other in our hotel room. We felt so far away, so helpless.

"She'll get to see Daddy," Sophie cried.

"I know!" I whimpered. "She's so lucky!" Which made us laugh.

We couldn't believe our year. At this point, Sophie had lost her dad. And now her fur-sister, Lucy. Everything seemed out of order and out of whack. I didn't want to admit to Sophie my guilt over not being there for Lucy because I didn't want Sophie to feel bad about our being in Paris. But I *was* guilt ridden—*I should have taken her to the vet before our trip!* I should have noticed she was in worse shape than I thought. We had only been gone for six days. *What if I had made these plans for the end of summer instead of the beginning?* Then we would have been home to take care of Lucy during her last hours.

And then a thought occurred to both Sophie and me. Maybe Lucy waited for us to leave to spare us another deathwatch. It sounded crazy. Lucy was a dog. How would she possibly orchestrate such a thing? But she was everything to us, as we were to her. She showed me how capable my heart was of expanding. She prepared me for Sophie.

We mourned Lucy in front of the Eiffel Tower that night. It gave both Sophie and me comfort to think that she and Joel were together. We also had a sense of humor about things. Death was something we were now quite familiar with. We had to laugh; our lives had become so ridiculous.

We left the next day for New York, where we'd be spending another week with my dad and Elisabeth and Holly and her kids in the Hamptons. Sophie and her cousins had a sibling-like bond that we all loved. They were all getting older, but with a three-year age range between them, they easily played together at the beach and in the pool. They put on shows for us after dinner, picked out movies to watch from the library. They took turns baking special treats with Grandma, while Grandpa "taught" them how to drive on the quiet backcountry roads. Our time together that summer was relaxed and familiar, but someone was missing. Particularly for Sophie and me, just like in Hawaii . . . and Chicago . . . and Paris. Our grief traveled with us.

I was dreading our return to Los Angeles.

I knew that without Joel and Lucy there to greet us, our house would seem even quieter. It was making me anxious. Sophie had a month before high school, and I wanted her to feel empowered and confident starting this new chapter. I tried to think of the things Joel would say to her or want to do with her, and I kept falling short. *I just didn't know!*

Sophie would be attending an academically rigorous public high school forty minutes from home. She would be taking a bus to school, and we'd have to be at the bus stop by 7:00 a.m. each morning. This would have been Joel's job. I questioned whether or not I should let the teachers know about her situation, that they'd have a new student who had recently lost a parent. While I had no problem announcing to the world that *I was a widow!*, Sophie was sensitive and self-conscious, and she wasn't sure she wanted her teachers to know. Like so many things, I wish I could have discussed this with Joel.

I feared that every decision I made would be the wrong one, that every action would be too fast or too slow or too late or too soon.

I also had no choice.

I've heard of helicopter parents and tiger mom parents and even snowplow parents. I felt that I was becoming a Bubble Wrap parent, wanting to protect Sophie from *any* kind of upset, even if the worst thing that could happen was already behind her. Of course, I failed miserably at this. She was a fourteen-year-old girl, and all the drama that comes along with that was out of my hands. There was social drama and school drama and family drama, and, oh yeah, her father had died. I knew Sophie's life was hers to live, no matter how hard I wanted to protect her.

"I think it may be time for you to start sleeping in your own room again, Smoosh," I told Sophie when we were back in Los Angeles.

She looked at me like she did when she was four and Joel and I had told her it was time to stop using her pacifier.

"Starting tonight?" she asked.

"Well," I said, "I just think that, you know, you're starting high school soon. We'll still do our reading and memory of Daddy every night—"

"I'm sort of . . . over that," she said carefully.

"Oh," I said. "I think it's important. It's hard to remember him sometimes. Hearing your thoughts helps me."

She looked at me. "I keep saying the same thing over and over. I feel like I don't remember that much so it makes me sad to try to think of something new." I felt the same way. Joel was starting to feel further away. Our memories were receding.

Joel was vegan for a second, right? Or was considering it, yes? He stopped eating red meat when Sophie did, but when did he stop eating chicken? And when he rode his bike to work, that was the summer he'd also race up the hills in the neighborhood, wasn't it? Or was that when he still had his office in Hollywood?

Sometimes it's the order of things that trips me up . . . *Did we buy that fancy blender before Joel was diagnosed with MS? Did we go to that party downtown for our anniversary, or was it around the holidays?* If I could hardly remember these things, how could I expect Sophie to? How could I honor Joel and give her a complete picture of who her dad was if I couldn't even remember when or if he was ever vegan? I wanted her more than anything to remember the *feeling* of Joel. It's one of the worst things about grief that no one prepared me for. You start to forget things about the people you love.

Joel hadn't even been gone a year. We were still living our year of firsts. We had experienced Thanksgiving and Hanukkah and the New Year. Sophie's birthday, Mother's Day, Sophie's middle school graduation, Father's Day. All without Joel. These things happened. We made plans, got ourselves dressed, showed up. I just don't know how.

His fifty-first birthday was approaching. I thought it was the perfect time to celebrate Joel in the same way we would have if he were alive. A party with Joel's favorite people, favorite music, in his favorite spot, our backyard. I invited everyone who would have been invited to Joel's birthday as if he were still alive and making the guest list himself. I then asked some of his friends to speak, to share *their* memories of Joel.

They all spoke of Joel's kindness and empathy. Agreed that he was a mensch of the highest order. One even acknowledged that seeing Joel interact with Sophie inspired him to have children of his own. Of course, they all talked about Joel's eclectic taste and knowledge of music. They admitted that they couldn't watch a Dodgers game without thinking of him. Joel was a good, caring friend with no pretense, no ego, and they were grateful to have known him.

Like with shiva, our house was full of friends that night. Seeing people who knew and loved Joel, hearing their stories, sharing our memories, all of these things kept Joel close and alive.

Sophie did sleep with me the night of Joel's birthday party. We read from our book of healing and shared a new memory, as we had done for the previous 260 nights.

"Tonight was nice," she said. "Daddy had a lot of friends."

I hugged her tight and said, "And a lot of people who loved him."

EIGHTEEN

Widowish

The first time I brought Marcos to a party, almost nine months after Joel died, a woman I knew from the neighborhood pulled me aside and said, "*You're here on a date?* Wait, when did your husband die again?"

The fact that I even went to a party, let alone with Marcos, was a big deal. That this exchange happened within five minutes of arriving had me feeling numb. I was a mix of nervousness and excitement being out in public with Marcos, but I didn't expect to feel so judged.

When I got the invitation to Mimi's birthday party a few weeks earlier, I called to tell her that I might bring someone with me.

"Sure!" she said. "Anyone you'd like; that's great!"

"I've . . . kind of been seeing someone. Someone you know."

"Oh my God, who?"

I took a deep breath and said, "Marcos."

She immediately started to laugh. Marcos taught guitar to both her kids. He was helping Mimi's daughter record songs for a demo she was making with her band.

"You know," she said. "I can see it, the two of you. The whole music connection." I could tell she was thinking it over. I could also tell she had a smile on her face. "I just can't wait to tell Paul!" she said, referring to her husband.

And that's how it started, my breaking the news to people that Marcos and I were dating. We'd be going to a party, and it would be our debut, in a way. I wanted my friends to be prepared to see me with someone other than Joel.

I devoted most of my time to Sophie that summer, but since we returned from our summer travels, Marcos and I had made a few plans that didn't necessarily include rushed time between the sheets.

Sophie still didn't know about him. I was still very much in mourning, and I didn't want Sophie, *or anyone*, to think that because I was dating Marcos, I missed or loved Joel any less. It would be a lot for my fourteen-year-old to understand even though I felt guilty keeping this from her.

When it felt "safe," Marcos would sometimes drive to my house, and we'd walk down to the boulevard for lunch or for drinks. He would often sing that Billy Joel song "Uptown Girl" when he saw me dressed for our date and in my end of the neighborhood.

"I see you now," he'd say if I was ordering a salade Niçoise and a glass of chardonnay. "I get your vibe."

He thought that I was "refined," and I liked that he would take me to his favorite Peruvian restaurant where the ceviche and *lomo saltado* were served on paper plates.

When I asked him if he was concerned about my being a widow—being too clingy, or too distant, or actively missing my husband, which I was—he'd say, "Sweetheart, I'm the man for the job."

I was more relaxed around him now, not as self-conscious as I had been originally. We would hold hands, and it felt nice to be out with him. Our relationship was evolving from a fling to a *thing*.

By now I had also told Ellie, who, when she met Marcos in his jeans and T-shirt, guitar in hand, said, "Well, he's not like the other dads."

My married neighbor Roxanne, who knew him through the food pantry, told me, "Oh, I'm in love with him, honey. If you don't date him, I will."

My friends who knew about Marcos were happy for me because they saw that I was *lighter*. They didn't worry about me as much. They liked that I wasn't alone and had someone to lean on.

A few friends, though, particularly those I knew through Joel, weren't thrilled. One husband seemed personally affronted by my new relationship. He thought it was too soon, and while he never said it out loud, I think he found it disrespectful. I tried to put myself in his shoes, tried to understand why it felt so personal to him.

Maybe I should slow down, I thought. *Put on the brakes, spend less time with Marcos and more time grieving Joel.* Only, I *was* still grieving. Marcos was a salve to all my sadness.

He asked a few times if it would be OK for Sophie to join us for a meal. I liked that he wanted to include her, but it felt a little too much, too soon. I had no one to ask for advice. This, like so many only parent/ young widow situations, was unchartered waters in my friend group. Even Allison couldn't offer the counsel I was looking for. "I can't believe it!" she'd say with a groan. "Joel's been gone a minute, and Brad's been gone four years. It's taking me forever to meet someone."

I was starting to feel compelled to tell Sophie about Marcos. A friend suggested that I use the word *date*. She thought this would soften the blow since a date seemed noncommittal and kind of casual. That didn't seem right to me, but I was at a loss. I didn't trust myself to just tell Sophie the truth. That Marcos and I had been seeing each other, plain and simple. But once I decided to tell her, I had to tell her immediately, like a confession. I was also a little giddy, the way one gets when in a new relationship.

I was on the phone with Jillian in my home office. "I'm going to tell Sophie about Marcos the minute we hang up. It's time, don't you think?"

"Yes, it's probably good that she knows. Especially now that you're telling people about him."

"And I'm going to that party with him next weekend. I just don't want her to hear it from someone else."

"Yeah, tell her. Then call me after and tell me what happened."

"OK," I said.

I put down my phone and heard Sophie in the kitchen.

"Smoosh?" I called to her. "Come in here for a sec?"

She came to the door. "What's up?"

I didn't prepare what to say and was so intent on telling her *that very second* that I just blurted it out.

"You won't believe it," I said. "Remember your guitar teacher, Marcos? He asked me out on a date!"

It was clumsy; my delivery was all wrong. It came out too fast.

Sophie stood in front of me and burst into tears. At the most, three seconds had elapsed. Her feelings were so raw, so immediate. Tears weren't just sliding down her cheeks, they were pouring. She turned red and started screaming, "That's disgusting! He knew Daddy! It's not right, Mom! You can always have another husband, but I'll never have another dad! I hate you, and I hate him!"

I tried to interject with "But I like that he knew Daddy!" and "Daddy's still my husband!" but I could barely get the words out. She stormed off, distraught, upset, angry.

I closed my eyes and sat there, my heart racing. I heard her bedroom door slam shut. If I felt bad about keeping this from her before, I felt even worse now. *How could I have been so stupid? So careless? So thoughtless?* I sat there crying.

I'm ruining Sophie's life!

I'm the worst mother in the world!

I can't do this alone!

I considered calling things off with Marcos, waiting to start dating until Sophie was in college. I sat in my office, searching for clarity by whispering to Joel.

I'm sorry, hun.

I fucked up, Joel.

I'm so sorry.

I kept waiting for Sophie's breakdown. I kept thinking that she was going to fall apart at some point, with the realization that Joel was forever gone. She was quiet about her grief, more private than I was. But this breakdown she was having was at *my* doing. I was the one causing this pain and I couldn't bear it.

And then I thought of Iyanla. She says asking for help and offering gratitude will help in any kind of crisis. I tried so hard to do both.

What do I do?

What should I do?

Thank you for telling me what to do!

But I didn't know who "you" was.

I couldn't get my mind to slow down. I had read somewhere that sometimes the best thing to do in a crisis is nothing. Nothing was about all I could handle. I was exhausted. I was sad. I was so angry with myself.

I went to my room, undressed, washed my face, and got in bed. I lay on my back, one hand on my heart, one on my belly. I inhaled deeply, exhaled deeply. I tried to make my mind quiet, but my heart felt so heavy. I got still and just kept breathing.

Inhale . . . exhale . . . inhale . . . exhale.

My mind slowed down. I thought of Joel. He's who I needed in that moment. I exhaled deeply and whispered to him.

Hun, I said. *I'm losing my mind, and I miss you. I don't know how I can live in this world without you.*

I took another breath.

I'm seeing Marcos. I kind of think you know that. Do you? Are you OK with it?

I was crying now.

I'm worried about Sophie. I need you here for her. I will be OK, I'm stronger than I thought. But Sophie needs you. I'm not enough for her on my own. I don't know how I'm going to do it.

And out of nowhere, these thoughts came into my head.

We will be OK.

Sophie knows I love her. She knows that Joel loves her.

Joel is with us. Joel is with us. Joel is here.

And in the stillness of my room, my face wet with tears, I opened my eyes, and I swear I heard Joel say to me, *"No matter what occurs, I will find you."*

I felt him. He found me at my lowest and showed up anyway.

I was getting dressed for Mimi's birthday party and still hadn't brought up Marcos to Sophie since the *date* debacle. It had been almost a full week, and neither of us said anything about it. We went about our lives, intertwined as we were, as if it never happened. But I didn't want more time to pass before bringing it up again, especially because I would be out with Marcos that night.

She was on the couch watching TV.

"What are you watching?" I asked.

"*Keeping Up with the Kardashians*."

"Oh," I said and sat next to her.

"Their dad died, too," she said. "When they were young."

"I know. Do they talk about him on the show?"

"All the time!" she said. "They just showed an episode with them watching home movies of him. It was sad, but good."

"That's really sweet," I said.

"I know. I want to watch my bat mitzvah video again."

We tried to watch it months earlier, but it was difficult. Seeing Joel again, struggling to walk but with a big smile on his face, hearing his voice; it felt tragic. We stopped the video less than halfway through.

"We'll definitely do that," I said. "Whenever you want."

People may make fun of the Kardashians, and I totally get that, but they also celebrate their father on his birthday and keep his memory alive in so many ways. They had survived his loss. It gave Sophie hope that she would survive Joel's, too.

I said to Sophie, "So. We don't have to talk about this right now, but I want you to know Marcos is going to be at Mimi's later."

She nodded. I said, "He's a good person, Smoosh."

"I don't hate him," she said quietly.

"Thank you for saying that," I said. "But even if you did, it would be OK. Your feelings are yours to have. But I like him very much, and I want you to understand that he will never replace Daddy. No one ever will."

She looked at me, her voice shaky. "I just miss him," she said.

I reached out and pulled her into my arms.

"I do, too," I said. "So much."

I held her tight.

"You know, I will always love Daddy. Always. No matter what."

She pulled away to look at me. "But what if you get married again?"

Marriage was the furthest thing from my mind.

"That won't be happening anytime soon," I assured her. "For real. And even if it does one day in the far, far, far away future, Daddy was there first. He's still my husband. He'll always be my husband. Even if I do get married again one day, Daddy is my forever husband."

"Really?" she asked.

"Really," I said. "And whoever I end up with, *if* I end up with anyone, will just have to accept it."

The woman at Mimi's party was waiting for me to answer her questions—
You're here on a date? Wait, when did your husband die again?

"Are *you* here on a date?" I asked.

She gave me a curious look. "Um . . . no."

"And how long ago was your divorce?"

She stammered, her face turning red. "Well . . . um . . . I mean . . ."

"Uh-huh," I said as I poured myself a drink. "So nice seeing you."

I walked away, knowing that behind me, she was reeling.

Actually, that's not what happened. Not at all. But in hindsight, I wish I had said those things.

In real life, I'm the one who stammered. I didn't even think to be snarky. I simply answered her question: "Almost nine months ago." I saw her considering this information. I then told her she looked *great* and walked away, self-conscious and nervous. I figured that she just said out loud what a lot of people were probably thinking.

There was an expectation about *The Widow.*

Am I sad enough?

Is it OK to see me smile?

Am I allowed to feel happy?

I felt like I was failing at widowhood. I missed my husband, but no one knew that when they looked at me. They just saw a mom with blonde highlights going to yoga, picking up her daughter from school, buying groceries at Trader Joe's. And now I was at a party with a date when I should have been home, grieving, all alone.

I didn't look like a widow. I wasn't acting like a widow. But I *felt* like a widow.

I guess I was just widow*ish.*

I looked for Marcos and found him in the center of a small crowd. They were all listening to him tell a story. He looked handsome in his brown corduroy blazer, holding a cocktail. He was smiling, and when he saw me, he lifted his arm and said, "There she is. There's my girl."

I was mortified. I was *his* girl?

It felt like a dream; I saw all of these faces turn toward me. They were the faces of people I knew casually for years. As I approached, someone reached out, touched my arm. "We're so happy for you!"

Another said, "He's adorable!"

One came close and whispered in my ear, "He looks like Joel."

I reached Marcos, and he put his arm around my shoulders and gave me a squeeze. Everyone laughed and smiled.

Marcos kissed my cheek. I turned pink and there was an audible "Awwww" from the people surrounding us.

This is too much. I can't.

I excused myself and went outside to the bar. I poured myself some vodka and drank it down. As I poured myself another, Marcos appeared by my side.

"Hey," he said. "You OK?"

I nodded yes. "It's just a lot."

"You want to stay, have another drink? Or if you want to leave, just let me know. I'm good either way. Whatever you want to do."

I looked at him. Like Joel, he was so *good*.

How did I get so lucky?

"Sweetheart?" Marcos said, eyebrows raised.

I put down my drink and put my hands on his face. I couldn't help it. It could have been the vodka, it could have been the moment. I kissed him, right on the lips, standing there in the backyard, in front of everyone.

Marcos may have sung "Uptown Girl" to me when I picked him up that night, but the song that was going through my mind was Bonnie Raitt's "Something to Talk About."

Marcos didn't mind one bit.

NINETEEN

Getting Personal

I n my writing group that week, I wrote a scene in my novel where one of the main characters goes on a horrible date with a guy she meets online. It was well received, and I decided that I would read it in our upcoming writer's salon.

As Leigh and I were walking to our cars that night, we talked about class and the things we were writing. Leigh and I were close, but we didn't have a lot of friends in common and I realized I hadn't told her about Marcos yet. I felt compelled to, especially since half the neighborhood saw us together at Mimi's party over the weekend.

"So how are you doing, sweetie?" Leigh asked.

"I'm seeing Marcos!" I blurted out.

She stopped walking and looked at me. "What?" she asked.

It was almost as clumsy as when I used the word *date* with Sophie.

"Marcos and I have been seeing each other," I said.

"Marcos . . . the musician Marcos?" she asked.

"Uh-huh."

Like everyone in our neighborhood, her kids had also taken guitar lessons from him.

"OK, wait a minute, let me absorb that." She started nodding and turned to face me. "You know," she said. "I just feel called to tell you something."

My guard immediately went up. Leigh spoke "universe" and when she *felt called*, I had to listen. I braced myself for what she was about to say.

"It's just . . ." She chose her words carefully. "I love the piece you wrote tonight. I love the whole novel you're writing. But I feel like Joel recently died. You're raising your daughter on your own. You're now telling me that you're seeing Marcos."

"So?" I said. I couldn't help but feel defensive.

"So I'd like to suggest that you start writing about what's going on for you personally. These characters in your novel, they will always be there. You can go back to them at any time."

"Uh-huh," I said, wondering where this was going.

"I say this simply for your consideration," Leigh continued. "If you were to write about the deep and meaningful emotional journey that you've been on, and will continue to be on for possibly even your whole life, I think it would not only be good for you, but good for others as well."

I stood there stunned. I just revealed a secret I had been carrying around, and she didn't have anything to say about it? Then she had the nerve to comment on my writing and what I *should* be writing instead? *I write fiction. I write make-believe. Why in the world would I ever even consider writing about my personal life?*

I got flustered, looking for my words. "Uh-huh. Well, I've never written about myself before. I'm not sure I want to."

"You may *think* you don't want to, but those are just thoughts. I'm just asking you to consider it," she said. "And as a side note, I love Marcos!"

She gave me a tight hug, then got into her car. "There's so much there, Melissa. Personal stories are powerful."

I stood there in the middle of the street and watched her drive away. As I turned to open my car door, out of nowhere, I opened my mouth and screamed. I wasn't expecting to, and it was a scream that was so loud and so fierce that I scared myself. I got in my car, opened up my sunroof, and looked up at the night sky.

I was so angry. Something about what Leigh said triggered me.

Write about my "emotional journey"? What the fuck?!

I rolled down all of the windows and let the cool air in.

Fuck her!

Fuck all of this shit!

Fuck Joel for dying!

Fuck my writing!

Fuck my life!

I felt the breeze on my skin as I drove down the hill. I didn't want to go home like this. I was too mad. Mad at Leigh for her stupid suggestion, mad at everyone for having an opinion on *my* life, mad at Joel for leaving me, and mad at Marcos for being so . . . for being so . . . I didn't know why I was mad at Marcos, but I was suddenly furious with him! So furious that instead of driving down the hill and making a left turn toward home, I made a right and headed straight for his house.

He happened to be outside, unloading his truck from a gig he had that day. He smiled when he saw me. I pulled up on the wrong side of the street, jumped out of my car, and approached him.

"Hey!" he said, his smile quickly fading when he saw me rushing him. "What's the matter? What's going on?"

I was breathing heavily, practically hyperventilating.

"Sweetheart?" he said.

"Don't call me 'sweetheart'!" I yelled.

"What happened. Did something happen?"

"I am so mad!" I yelled. "I can't take it!"

I heard Joel's voice say, "What can you take?" It stopped me cold.

"What?" I said to the air.

Marcos started to say, "I don't know what's happening here but—"

"Shh!" I yelled. I kept turning around, looking for Joel. "Hun?"

"Huh?" Marcos said.

"Who said that?" I demanded.

It was nighttime. The sky was dark. But I swear, in this moment, I was blinded by the sun. Or what I thought was the sun. I know that I was staring at Marcos. I know that we were standing in front of his house. It may have been my headlights that were blinding me, but I felt the need to squint. That's when I saw Joel standing there, smiling, happy, the way he was when I saw him on the bridge in my dream.

"Oh my God, hun," he was saying, laughing. "You're losing it."

"I really am," I said.

We stared at each other. I couldn't believe it.

"You," he said.

I sighed. "I miss you."

"I'm right here," he said. But I didn't know if it was Joel saying that. Or Marcos.

I felt my face wet with tears. I was so tired of crying. I was so tired of feeling all of my feelings, all the time.

"Hey," Marcos said, approaching me, hands up in surrender. "Let's go inside. I think you need to sit down. Or maybe I should drive you home."

It was dark out again. Marcos was reaching out for me, and over his shoulder, I saw Joel. He held up his hand in a wave. His eyes were twinkling. He looked healthy. He was smiling.

"Don't go!" I whispered.

"I'm right here," he said. That time, I knew it was Marcos.

He looked into my eyes. He wiped my tears with his thumbs. "Hey," he said. "It's OK. You're going to be OK."

He took my hand. "Come on, sweetheart, let's get you home."

I wrapped my fingers in his and wiped my face with our clasped hands. He laughed.

"Sorry," I said.

"For what?"

"Being such a mess, I guess."

"Hey," he said. "Don't apologize. I'm a blues musician, baby. I sing the blues, I play the blues, I *feel* the blues."

He sort of sang that last part, and I shook my head wearily—this was so Marcos. What did his being a blues musician have anything to do with anything?

"I feel crazy," I said, "but you may actually *be* crazy."

"I am crazy," he said. "Crazy about you . . . because I love you."

"What?" I said.

"Does that help you feel better? At all? Maybe a little bit?" he asked.

I looked at this brown-eyed, soulful, truly good man standing in front of me. *He must be the one the psychic told me about, right?* He had a son. And even if he had never said it out loud, I knew he loved me, because I felt it.

Marcos often made no sense to me. As a couple, we made even less sense. We lived on "different sides" of the boulevard and occupied what seemed like two different worlds at times. But he was so open, so ready to take me in. Me *and* my widowed heart.

He stood in front of me, so happy, even though I was a wreck.

"I don't know what to do with you," I said.

"Do nothing then. Just receive, sweetheart. Think you can do that?" And then we kissed. My anger, sadness, and anxiety dissipated every time our lips touched. It didn't matter that I felt so broken and overwhelmed and confused, so confused all the time . . . Marcos accepted me as I was.

I slept alone that night. Sophie was in her room; I was in mine. I read my passage from *Healing After Loss* by myself and said my memory with my eyes closed, picturing Joel on the sidewalk that night.

As I went about my life and routines that week, Leigh's words bounced around inside my head, as much as I tried to ignore them.

Driving Sophie to school, I'd hear Leigh telling me, *Personal stories are powerful!*

Paying bills and writing checks, her words echoed: *Write about the deep and meaningful emotional journey that you've been on!*

Cooking. Every. Single. Meal. The words *Start writing about what's going on for you personally* played over and over in my mind.

I also pictured Marcos. On the sidewalk. In the dark. Professing his love for me . . . while Joel stood just over his shoulder.

I wanted so badly to resist Leigh's suggestion. It felt *so personal.* Joel was mine. He belonged to me and Sophie. I didn't want to share him, not at all. And how would I even be able to write about Marcos? I was still processing all of it. I had nothing figured out . . . But I couldn't stop writing in my head. I had so much to say on the subject of widowhood. Not just what I was feeling on the inside, but the way I was perceived as a widow in the world . . . the things people said to me, the things I said to them . . .

By the time I got to class that week, I was bursting. When we finished our meditation and went over some writing prompts, my fingers flew across my computer keyboard in a way that I can only describe as otherworldly. I wasn't even aware that I was writing so when the timer went off, I was shocked to see that I had written close to ten pages. Single spaced. In a small font. What I had written was personal, intense, and it was all true. I sat there and sobbed while reading it aloud to my classmates. I appreciated their patience as I choked and shnorkled over every sentence. So much for being the only "professional" writer in the class.

For the next six weeks and the whole following session, I wrote about Joel and the MS. About the confusion in the hospital. About the day he died. About his ashes, and the dogs, and shiva. I wrote about Sophie and feeling the weight of responsibility as an only parent. I wrote about our neighbors and our neighborhood and our friends. I wrote about the depths of my sadness and how my heart was broken and expanding at the same time. Once I started writing personally, about all that I was experiencing, I couldn't stop. The writing was cathartic, it was healing, it has been the thing that has saved me the most. The best part is, in writing about Joel, it keeps him close and alive.

And even though I was *feeling* love for Marcos, I couldn't admit it to him or myself before I made Sophie fully aware of our relationship. By now, he and I were a real couple. It just happened, and I just let it happen.

Sophie had started high school, and we had made the transition to those early morning rides to the bus and new friends, and all that comes with being in a new school at fourteen years old. On occasion, I would allude to Marcos, but it would always be a casual mention.

By the way, I saw Marcos for coffee today, and don't forget, Smoosh, you need to bring your French book to school tomorrow.

But I was ready to help her understand that Marcos and I were more than friends. It was the evening of the freshman dance at Sophie's school. Her friends and their moms were coming over to get ready at our house.

I had made some snacks for the girls as they got dressed in the living room. Some of the moms and I were hanging out in the kitchen. There was perfume and makeup and giggles, lots of giggles . . . and then the doorbell rang.

One of the girls rushed to answer it, thinking it was another friend arriving, but it was Marcos. Her mouth dropped open.

"Um," she called to Sophie. "Why is Marcos here?"

"Hello, young lady," Marcos said to Sophie's friend, all smiles.

Sophie came running out and saw Marcos in the doorway.

"Hey, Sophie, how are you?"

Sophie quickly turned to look at me. I steadied myself for her response. She could have started crying or yelling or acting mortified.

But she did none of those things. She turned to her friend and said, "Oh, he and my mom are dating."

The friend's eyes got wide. She shared a look with her mother, who was in the kitchen, and got teary-eyed. She mouthed to me, *So happy for you!*

Sophie ran to the door. "Hi, Marcos," she said. "Come in."

"I'm not staying long," he said. "Just wanted to say hi."

The next few minutes played out like an episode of *Wild Kingdom*, where one species (the teenage girls) crowds around to observe a lone member of another species (Marcos). The young girls were in a group whispering and giggling and pointing to Marcos, while he stood there taking it. The girls then broke apart and, thankfully, went back to getting ready.

By now, Marcos had joined me in the kitchen.

"Hi, sweetheart," he said. He gave me a kiss on the cheek and acknowledged the other moms. He knew all of them, who behind his back were nodding their approval and giving me the thumbs-up.

Every so often, one brave girl would poke her head out and say, "Hi, Marcos!"

After a few minutes, I went back to the living room to check on things and pulled Sophie aside.

"You OK with all of this, Smoosh?" I asked.

"Yeah, it's fine," she said. "Can I borrow your mascara?"

"Mascara?" I said, feigning shock.

"Please?" Sophie asked, smiling.

I gave her a quick kiss and watched as she ran back to her friends, business as usual.

TWENTY

Love

O h, I think that's just wonderful!" Hal said over brunch. He and Rita were taking me out for my birthday. Which meant we were approaching the first-year anniversary of Joel's passing.

I loved celebrating my birthday. In our family, birthdays are like national holidays. So when Hal called to ask if there was something special I'd like to do, I quickly and happily said yes and made a brunch reservation for Hal, Rita, and myself at a trendy new restaurant nearby. We were toasting another trip around the sun for me, but we had Joel on our minds. It was comforting being with Hal because we both, miraculously, were surviving a life without Joel.

Losing Joel brought us closer together. We bonded during the countless hours we spent in the hospital, and we had been through this excruciating loss together. We respected each other and the pain, suffering, and, ultimately, survival that we had experienced. We were war buddies. Running mates.

Once we had our champagne flutes in hand and put in our orders for salmon benedict and chicken-sausage scrambles, I said, "So I want you both to know that I'm seeing someone."

Rita's eyes widened. "Oh, that's terrific! I'm so happy to hear that."

Hal looked stunned at first, but it was a happy stunned. He smiled, looked over at Rita, then raised his glass to me. "Oh, I think that's just wonderful!" We clinked our glasses, and I cried. Not the ugly, tears-pouring-down-my-face crying that I was so accustomed to, but a soft, mist-of-tears kind of cry because I was so happy that they were happy. I had a feeling they would be. They loved me. They knew how hard it was for me to act *as if* I had a life without Joel. But they saw me doing it. They saw how I was parenting for two, on my own, and I knew they were relieved when they heard that I had a respite from it all.

"So tell us," Hal said. "Who's the lucky guy?"

I told them about Marcos. How he used to teach Sophie guitar and was also a working musician with gigs all over town. How he was a do-gooder in the community and also had a teenage son. When I got to the part about him and Joel knowing each other, Hal's whole face lit up.

"That's great!" he said. "Isn't that something?"

"When can we meet him?" Rita asked, excited.

The conversation continued. There was no judgment. No criticism.

If anyone was watching us from across the room, they'd observe the two of them, a couple, sitting on one side of the booth, while I sat alone, across from them, an empty seat next to me. It looked like someone was missing. But Joel was with us. We all felt it.

When I called to invite Joel's mother, Nancy, to a pub near her house to hear a friend of mine play guitar one night, she immediately said yes. Nancy was always open to a new experience and meeting new people.

"I just want to let you know ahead of time, the person who'll be performing is a man I've been seeing."

"I figured," she said, laughing. "Why else would you be inviting me? Otherwise, it would just be about the food."

When Nancy showed up, Marcos had already started performing, so she sat with me and we watched him.

"He's so handsome!" she said. "I love his nose."

This made me laugh. Nancy was always one who marched to her own rhythm. I appreciated that she didn't balk or wince or take any issue whatsoever that Marcos and I were a couple. When he took a break and came over to our table, Nancy stood up and hugged him.

"I know you're a good person or Melissa wouldn't be spending time with you."

"Thank you," Marcos said. "I think she's a good person, too."

"Of course she is!" Nancy said. "It's very nice to meet you, Marcos. Really nice."

My in-laws have embraced Marcos fully. I went from being their daughter-in-law to something even closer. A daughter-in-feeling. Hal and Rita invite Marcos to family dinners. Nancy shows up for his gigs, usually in the front row, and oftentimes she'll bring her friends.

I don't know that we're a modern family, but we're a unique family. A motley crew kind of family. The kind of family that people, when they meet us, can't quite figure out who belongs to who, unless Sophie is with us, and then it's an easy: "These are Sophie's grandparents, I'm her mother, and Marcos is my boyfriend." It still seems complicated, but for us, we are simply family.

I threw myself a birthday party that first year. It was a birthday celebration and a let's-get-together-and-remember-Joel party. I wanted to celebrate life, knowing that it can sometimes be cut short. I bought a new dress, ordered food from my favorite restaurant, stocked up with plenty of booze, and gave Marcos the job of bartender. I could tell he was nervous. Marcos is a confident man, but there was some unspoken pressure about this gathering. It would be the first time that many of my friends, and Joel's, would be meeting him. In my house, the one I shared with Joel, in the same kitchen where Joel and I had hosted so many events.

"Sweetheart," Marcos said when he arrived with ice and limes. "Just put me where you need me, and I'll do whatever you tell me to."

I took him in. He was not the man I thought he was those few years ago when I met him outside his house for Sophie's guitar lesson. He was so much more.

"Thank you," I said. "Thank you. Thank you." I kissed him.

"For what?" he asked.

"For being here. It can't be easy for you, and I appreciate it. Thank you. I love you."

I half expected him to say *you*. But that wasn't our thing, or my thing anymore.

We kissed and he said, "It's all good, baby. Love. L-O-V-E. Love."

"Love?" I said.

"Yes, sweetheart. Love."

And that's how *love* became our shorthand. *Our* call and response.

The doorbell rang, Jillian was the first to arrive. She saw Marcos in the kitchen and did a double take.

"I thought he was Joel for a second," she said, pulling me aside.

"I know," I said. "I think that's going to happen a lot tonight."

She looked around. "Does the dog like him?"

"She's not barking," I said.

"Then it's fine. I'm happy for you. Happy birthday!"

And that's how the night went. It *was* weird. We were all doing double takes. But Marcos went with it. Friends were curious about him. Some interviewed him over cocktails; others made small talk. He lit the birthday candles on my cake and carried it over to me to make a wish. My friends stood around and sang. My wishes were so different this year than last. When Joel was in a coma, I wished for him to be free. That year, and every year since, I wished for Joel to stay close.

Five days later, on the day that marked one year since Joel's death, Sophie and I sat on the beach in Malibu and ate his favorite candy. We shared some funny memories of him and reflected on the year. We cried looking at photos in an album I had made, amazed that we made it this far without him.

"I don't know how I should feel," Sophie said. "It's like I miss Daddy, but I don't feel sad all the time. Sometimes I think I should."

"I don't think Daddy would want you to be sad all the time. In fact, I don't think he'd want you to be sad at all."

"Of course, I'm going to be sad, Mom. My dad died!"

"I know!" I said. "And he loved you so much!" I tried to formulate another sentence, but I didn't know what to say. So I went to my usual. "I think you just need to feel your feelings, whenever you have them, you know? And whatever you feel, even if it's not sad, that's OK. Even on a day like today."

People kept asking me what Sophie and I were going to do that day, on the anniversary. It put pressure on us. Like with Father's Day and Joel's birthday and our wedding anniversary. I've come to learn that my feelings are unpredictable. It could be a Tuesday in January, and I'll feel inconsolable. But when Joel's birthday comes around in August, I could be feeling cheerful. There's no rhyme or reason to grief. It hits you when it hits you. I tried to convey this to Sophie, although that day at the beach, at year one, I was still learning this myself.

"I think we just need to honor Daddy every day. However we can. And however we feel, we feel."

"I feel lucky," Sophie said.

"About what?"

"That you and Daddy . . . you loved each other. So many of my friends' parents don't anymore. But that's a memory I'll always have. That you and Daddy were happy together."

"Yup," I said. "We were. We were a happy little family, all of us."

"We still are," she said.

I smiled at my girl, locked her arm in mine, and the two of us sat there on the beach and stared out at the ocean, together.

TWENTY-ONE

God Laughs

Sometimes I imagine Joel on the basketball court. He's sweaty, running, happy. He moves easily. He makes a block, grabs the ball, dribbles it down the court, and shoots a basket, scoring one for his team. I don't know where this is, I can't make out the other players, but the sun is shining, there is a slight breeze, and Joel looks and feels healthy. He is moving, he is happy, he is free.

I have finally been able to leave the hospital. I can now envision Joel as he was, and how he might have been if not for the MS, if not for the West Nile virus.

I discuss this with the two widows sitting next to me at Allison's house. It's a relief to remember my husband free of illness and distress. They understand this completely. We are comfortable speaking this language of grief and healing, and we speak it freely.

"Were your husbands athletic?" I ask.

"Dan played some sports in high school, but as an adult, he was more of a runner. It was his thinking time," one of them says.

"And Mike wasn't really into sports. He was into cheesecake. Is cheesecake a sport?"

We laugh, the three of us, and I excuse myself to talk to Allison in the kitchen.

"Such a great turnout!" she says.

"I can't believe it!"

We both take in the group gathered in Allison's living room. About ten widows, and three widowers.

"I think we can get started soon," I tell Allison.

She nods yes, and we turn toward this group we've assembled.

~

Had I known when I was younger that this would be how my life ended up, I never would have believed it. But then again, I wouldn't have believed so many things:

That Joel and I would end up married didn't seem possible until he came to Seattle and found me.

That we would have only one child when we wanted so many wasn't expected either, but our family ended up being perfect exactly the way it was.

That we wouldn't grow old together never crossed my mind.

I never expected to be a widow in my midforties.

I also never expected to fall in love with my daughter's guitar teacher.

They say if you want to make God laugh, tell Her your plans. I may have never uttered my plans out loud, but She is laughing anyway.

When I meet up with friends whom I haven't seen in a while, and they ask how I'm doing, I'll usually start with, *I miss Joel*. It's hard not to cry in those moments. To this day, *so many years later*, I still say to those closest to me, *Can you believe it? That this is my life?* And they all say the same thing . . . *No. I can't.*

What was so surreal in the early days of losing Joel is now simply reality, but still just as hard to fathom. Managing my grief has gotten easier, but I'm still grieving. I don't think that ever stops. It just gets easier, since time, I've learned, is a miraculous healer.

While Marcos and I have no plans to live together anytime soon, we have discussed it. Things seem to work for us as they are, as unconventional as our relationship is. We agree that maintaining separate homes could be the key to our success. One time when we spoke about the possibility of living together, Marcos said, "You'll bring your books and your music. We'll have a shelf for Joel . . ." He accepts that Joel occupies a huge space in Sophie's and my hearts, and that the shrine I have of Joel is coming with me wherever I go. I love him for that.

The shrine that sits on the shelf of my walk-in closet consists of a sealed bowl with some of his ashes. A photo of Joel taken at the Dodgers game the day he caught that fly ball. Next to that photo is the actual baseball, which is sealed in a see-through plastic box and has the date of the game in Joel's handwriting on it. There's another photo of Joel, Sophie, and me, all hugging our dog Lucy, from a day at a park. A purple magic fairy wand filled with stars and sparkles that Sophie liked to play with when she was a baby is there, too. I see these things every day. I make sure to take them all in.

It took some time, but Sophie and Marcos have forged a meaningful relationship. He is respectful and understanding of our memories of Joel, and Sophie appreciates it as much as I do. Marcos accepts that there is no replacing Joel, or even filling in for him. He provides unconditional support for our mother-daughter dynamic duo.

When Sophie had trouble passing her driving test the first time around, Marcos took over teaching her to drive and took her to the DMV for her next driving test. I stood at home pacing, staring at the clock, imagining every worst-case scenario.

"Sweetheart?" Marcos said when I picked up the phone. "She got the lady in the Hawaiian shirt."

"Oh my God, no!" I yelled. There were rumors that this particular DMV was an easy pass, unless, of course, you got the Hawaiian shirt–wearing lady as your tester.

Marcos laughed. "It's OK," he said. "She's in line now."

"What line?" I asked, my heart pounding outside of my chest.

"The line where they take the picture. For the license. She passed."

That Marcos didn't begin the conversation with the good news was typical. But it didn't matter. I sighed with relief and fell to my knees in tears. When we hung up, I picked up my favorite framed photo of Joel. "She did it, hun. Our baby girl is driving now. If you're not sitting with her every time she gets behind the wheel, I will kill you!"

I started publishing essays about my widow*ish* journey online and in local newspapers. I began hearing from so many people. My story had resonated with them and their emails had common themes:

"No one understands my story."

"My parents want to help but the only widows they know are in their seventies."

"I'm still young enough to get married again, maybe even have more kids, but no one wants to date a widow."

Many of them lived in Los Angeles. A few of them asked if they could meet me. They didn't know of any widows their same age. They wanted to share their stories. So I called Allison. "I think we need to do something about all these young widows."

"Yes!" she said. "Let's plan our first meeting. I'm happy to volunteer my backyard if everyone brings some food. We'll make it a potluck."

"With wine!" I said.

"Absolutely!" she agreed.

I was nervous sending out that first email. There were so many people on the list! Many lived close by, some were friends of friends. I wanted to strike the right tone, make sure people knew that it wasn't a bereavement group but a social gathering among people who understood . . . I barely hit send when the replies came back fast and eager. People were so thankful. They wanted to connect, to meet and embrace this strange widow*ish* world that we all inhabit.

I hold Allison back before we head into her living room. I give her a quick hug.

"Thank you!" I say.

"You're welcome," she says. "But for what, I don't know."

"For calling me that day. For reaching out. I didn't think I would call you back, but I'm so glad I did."

"Yup. And look at us now!"

I look toward the living room and take a deep breath, then Allison and I head in the direction of the group we've assembled.

For the first few meetings, I asked everyone to bring a picture of their spouse who died. We all went around, introduced ourselves, and our loved one. I brought the picture of Joel that five-year-old Sophie took— *I'm Melissa. This is my husband, Joel.*

We all shared a memory. *Joel made me laugh out loud every day. Early on, he told me a joke about John Cougar Mellencamp.*

I told them that on the way over, I saw a hummingbird. One of the widows immediately said, "My girls and I know that every butterfly we see is a visit from Peter."

Another widow chimed in. "And every passing fire truck is Stewart saying hi to our three-year-old son."

We get together several times a year. Each time we meet, there is a new member. We always honor the spouse we have lost. At every single meeting, we laugh, and we cry.

We share our stories over cabernet and brie and store-bought brownies. We are a surprisingly happy group—and young. Most of us, both men and women, lost our spouses in our forties, if not younger. If a stranger were to walk into our meeting, they would probably guess we were a book club, or colleagues from the office, or parents planning a school event. Not a group of widows.

We are all widow*ish*. No one "looks" like a widow. If we wear black, it's because it's on trend. You don't see any gray hair because we color it. Some of us are in relationships, and some help write each other's online dating profiles. Those of us with children are all *only parents* now, and we have kids ranging in age from preschool to college.

We are in this surreal club because of cancer, because of failing hearts, because of brain tumors, because of tragedy.

And one of us is in this club because of a mosquito bite.

That would be me.

This is my story.

ACKNOWLEDGMENTS

This book became a reality when my agent, Caryn Karmatz Rudy, offered me her condolences *and* representation on our first phone call. Her belief in my story as well as her intelligence and calm demeanor has meant the world to me—I feel so lucky to have found you!

I have pinched myself over and over for having "a book in production." Thanks to the entire team at Little A for making it such a joyful experience! It started with two amazing editors: Erin Callahan Mooney, whose early support I so appreciate, and Carmen Johnson, whose keen insights and genuine enthusiasm for *Widowish* have guided me thoughtfully through every part of this process.

I give Robin Finn credit for seeing what was possible long before I could even imagine it. Thank you for your continual support, love, and friendship. You are a light in the world even if it took me twelve years to notice!

Bella Mahaya Carter—you provided the safest space for me to start telling my story. I'm also in awe of the other writers I wrote with week in and week out . . . Keep going, all of you!

Courtney Churchill Crane and Megan Austin Oberle—my beloved *Ladies Who Lit*—I adore writing, sharing, and reading with both of you!

Clark Benson, Benjie Gordon, and Vince Hans, I am beyond grateful for your generosity . . . I know that Joel is, too.

I didn't realize it at the time, but my healing journey began when I received *Healing After Loss: Daily Meditations for Working Through Grief* by Martha Whitmore Hickman. Thank you, Darren Swimmer, for such a meaningful gift.

Chrisa Sadd, my beautiful friend whom I met on the same day as Joel—you will always have a special place in my heart.

Suzanne LaCock Browning, Michellene Debonis, Karen Gold, Visi Mooradian, Michelle Peterson, and Jennie Rosenthal—you were beacons of light during the darkest time. I love you all!

Gayle Abrams—my wonderful friend, you helped make sense of the craziness in the hospital (and Hollywood long before that!) with both your kind heart and detective skills.

Craig Rosen, Joel's friend since Hebrew school and my Jewish brother, you have been my memory when my own has failed. Our shared experiences with and about Joel help keep him alive, and that is everything.

Thanks to Melissa Hufjay McAlevey, Carolyn Prousky, and David Wild, who all encouraged me to continue sharing my story from the very beginning.

There is no better Widow Ambassador in the world than Susan Berin. Thank you for everything, Suzy. (When we met, Frank and Joel did, too, and that makes my heart smile . . .)

In addition to being the best first reader of every single word I've ever written, Ellie Miller is also the best friend, travel companion, cheerleader, and partner a girl could ask for (Joel approves).

I share everything in my life (even soda cans) with Stephanie Levine. She is the Gayle to my Oprah (and sometimes the other way around). Even after we've talked for hours, we always have more to say to each other . . . and I appreciate Susan Levison for understanding this.

To my much older and beautiful sissy—no one makes me laugh like you do, even when I'm crying. *You're terrible . . .*

Thank you to *all* of my parents for a lifetime of love and support: *Mom*, you have always encouraged me and been my biggest fan. *Dad*, your love of reading and inquisitive nature probably turned me into a writer (and thanks for making me feel like your favorite daughter even though my sister really is!). *Schatzi*, I don't know how any of us would manage without you—you keep us all sane!

To Joel's family . . . thank you all for your unconditional love and acceptance, and for raising the man I will love forever. I am so grateful for all of you.

To my blues-playing, do-gooder, Luis Oliart . . . you are and have been the man for the job. Love, baby.

Sophie, you are my world! Joel's goodness lives in you and that is the *Best Thing Ever*. I will always be as besotted with you as the day you were born. Everything is for you, Smoosh.

To the many widows and widowers I have met over the years, your stories and memories matter. Thank you for sharing them with me. It is a privilege to bear witness. I wish you all continued healing, and love, which lives forever.

ABOUT THE AUTHOR

Melissa Gould's essays have appeared in the *New York Times*, the *Los Angeles Times*, the *Washington Post, Huffington Post, Buzzfeed*, and more. She's an award-winning screenwriter whose credits include *Bill Nye, the Science Guy; Party of Five; Beverly Hills, 90210*; and *Lizzie McGuire*. She lives in Los Angeles, California. Find out more about Melissa at https://widowish.com.